MAKE IT SNOW

MAKE IT SNOW

**FROM ZERO TO BILLIONS: HOW SNOWFLAKE
SCALED ITS GO-TO-MARKET ORGANIZATION**

**DENISE PERSSON
CHRIS DEGNAN**

WILEY

Copyright © 2026 by John Wiley & Sons, Inc. All rights reserved, including rights for text and data mining and training of artificial technologies or similar technologies.

Published by John Wiley & Sons, Inc., Hoboken, New Jersey.
Published simultaneously in Canada.

No part of this publication may be reproduced, stored in a retrieval system, or transmitted in any form or by any means, electronic, mechanical, photocopying, recording, scanning, or otherwise, except as permitted under Section 107 or 108 of the 1976 United States Copyright Act, without either the prior written permission of the Publisher, or authorization through payment of the appropriate per-copy fee to the Copyright Clearance Center, Inc., 222 Rosewood Drive, Danvers, MA 01923, (978) 750-8400, fax (978) 750-4470, or on the web at www.copyright.com. Requests to the Publisher for permission should be addressed to the Permissions Department, John Wiley & Sons, Inc., 111 River Street, Hoboken, NJ 07030, (201) 748-6011, fax (201) 748-6008, or online at http://www.wiley.com/go/permission.

The manufacturer's authorized representative according to the EU General Product Safety Regulation is Wiley-VCH GmbH, Boschstr. 12, 69469 Weinheim, Germany, e-mail: Product_Safety@wiley.com.

Trademarks: Wiley and the Wiley logo are trademarks or registered trademarks of John Wiley & Sons, Inc. and/or its affiliates in the United States and other countries and may not be used without written permission. All other trademarks are the property of their respective owners. John Wiley & Sons, Inc. is not associated with any product or vendor mentioned in this book.

Limit of Liability/Disclaimer of Warranty: While the publisher and author have used their best efforts in preparing this book, they make no representations or warranties with respect to the accuracy or completeness of the contents of this book and specifically disclaim any implied warranties of merchantability or fitness for a particular purpose. No warranty may be created or extended by sales representatives or written sales materials. The advice and strategies contained herein may not be suitable for your situation. You should consult with a professional where appropriate. Further, readers should be aware that websites listed in this work may have changed or disappeared between when this work was written and when it is read. Neither the publisher nor authors shall be liable for any loss of profit or any other commercial damages, including but not limited to special, incidental, consequential, or other damages.

For general information on our other products and services or for technical support, please contact our Customer Care Department within the United States at (800) 762-2974, outside the United States at (317) 572-3993 or fax (317) 572-4002.

Wiley also publishes its books in a variety of electronic formats. Some content that appears in print may not be available in electronic formats. For more information about Wiley products, visit our website at www.wiley.com.

Library of Congress Cataloging-in-Publication Data is Available:

ISBN: 9781394254200 (Cloth)
ISBN: 9781394254217 (ePub)
ISBN: 9781394254224 (ePDF)

Cover Design: Wiley
Author Photos: Courtesy of Chris Degnan,
Courtesy of Denise Persson

SKY10124706_082625

Contents

Foreword by Mike Speiser — vii

Phase I — Stealth — 1
Chapter 1 — Embed Sales and Culture Early into Your Startup — 3
Chapter 2 — Develop Your Sales Strategy — 15
Chapter 3 — Hiring and Deploying Your First Sales Reps — 27
Chapter 4 — Target One Competitor, for Now — 41
Chapter 5 — Scaling with Partners — 53
Chapter 6 — Scale Your Culture — 61

Phase II — Build — 71
Chapter 7 — Enter Marketing — 73
Chapter 8 — The Five Pillars of Marketing — 91
Chapter 9 — Advance Your Sales Team — 107

Chapter 10 Absolute Alignment Between Marketing and Sales	119
Chapter 11 From Product to Platform	133
Phase III Scale	**137**
Chapter 12 Hiring, Retention, and Parting Ways	139
Chapter 13 Build for a Billion	149
Chapter 14 Bottom-Up Sales	163
Chapter 15 Scaling a Data-Driven Marketing Organization	173
Chapter 16 Going Global	191
Chapter 17 Alignment for the Ages	207
Acknowledgments	*215*
Index	*219*

Foreword

"It's like one brain in two bodies."
—Mike Speiser on Chris Degnan and Denise Persson

IF YOU'RE SELLING to eight billion people, like Apple, marketing is the lead and sales follows marketing. If you're selling enterprise software, and you have tens of thousands of customers, sales is the driver and marketing serves sales. In either case, there has to be absolute alignment between these two organizations in order to be successful. Every great marketer I've met understands they must have a great relationship with sales. But a lot of marketers don't. The standout sales professionals I've met believe the same, but a lot of them don't work in lockstep with marketing.

Chris Degnan and Denise Persson worked side by side at Snowflake for nearly nine years. Theirs is one of the longest working relationships between a company's chief revenue officer and its chief marketing officer. It all began when Chris arrived in 2013—one year after Snowflake's inception. Denise arrived in 2016, when the company had just over 100 employees and annual revenues of about $3 million. Over the years, Snowflake would surge to more than 9,000 employees and $3 billion in annual sales. Along the way, it has delivered the largest software IPO in history, among many other industry milestones. Chris and Denise, and their growing organizations, have been there, in perfect alignment, delivering one sonic boom after another.

Hundreds of books exist about how to sell. The same amount exists on how to market. Many of these books deliver great strategies and some go further to guide organizations on how to execute. But there's nothing I've read that explains why these two organizations should be in perfect alignment, how to create and deliver on such a relationship, and what could happen to your company once you accomplish this.

Why should you learn about this from Denise and Chris? Snowflake's competitors are the largest technology companies in the world and have dominated their industries for decades: Google, Microsoft, Amazon Web Services, and others. Snowflake has successfully sold and marketed with and against them. Denise and Chris have also helped steer Snowflake through the COVID-19 pandemic and have served under all three of Snowflake's CEOs, who operate vastly different from one another. Frank Slootman joined in 2019 and brought the company to IPO a year later. Upon his arrival, he swapped out most c-level executives who would report to him, but not Chris and Denise.

Chris was hired to jump-start the sales organization. He was made a director, not a CRO. He had never before operated a large sales organization and was told from the very beginning that Snowflake would hire someone above him, eventually. When Frank and his CFO Mike Scarpelli arrived to Snowflake, they tested Chris to see if he could grow revenue and drive profitability for what would become a multibillion-dollar company. Frank is a sophisticated operations person but Chris passed each test. He hired a head of North America sales who reported to him—a person who had more experience than him. He split the sales organization into enterprise and commercial teams, and he hired people who operated at a bigger scale than he ever had. And he kept blowing out the sales numbers every quarter. If we hadn't tested him, if we hadn't pushed him, Chris wouldn't have become Chris. He just kept killing it, over and over.

Denise was already a seasoned executive, having been a CMO twice before joining Snowflake. She is one of the best, if not the best, CMOs I've ever seen. She is exceptional because marketing is tough. It's not one function, it's really five functions. Product marketing is different from field marketing. Brand marketing is different from lead generation, and so on. And it's a very tough job to get world-class people to lead these areas. It's more like being a CEO, and her organization is extraordinary in so many things that are fundamentally different from one another. She has an ability to find people who are exceptional for each of those functions.

Never has Chris said, "I generate all of the sales and I'm the more critical person." Denise had been in more senior roles before she arrived and had a wider breadth of responsibility. A lot of people like that have big egos and have trouble saying to sales, "I'm going to serve you." That's not Denise. In her interview with Chris, she said: "You are my customer."

Chris and Denise have absolute incredible trust. Never in the history of Snowflake, since I've known both of them, has Denise ever said anything critical of Chris, privately or publicly. And never has Chris said anything critical of Denise. They may get frustrated with another human but they understand how important it is to have trust. They make it look effortless, and that takes a lot of work. They always came to board meetings together and finished each other's sentences. It was like one brain in two bodies. Snowflake would not be Snowflake without Denise and Chris.

Read this book and you will learn how to accomplish many things in sales and marketing that have made Snowflake wildly successful from a startup to an industry powerhouse. You will learn that and much more—how to align two critical areas of an organization to deliver more than they deliver on their own. So sit down, lock in, and enjoy.

—**Mike Speiser**

PHASE I

Stealth

1

Embed Sales and Culture Early into Your Startup

"Holy crap! What have I done?"

—Chris Degnan

THEY SAY IT's better to have never flown first class then to have flown it and then be shuffled back to economy. That was my young life in a nutshell. I grew up in an upper-middle-class family. My father was a stockbroker when the market crashed in 1988. As I entered high school, we went from front row seats at Celtics games to a divorced family and my dad headed to prison. I had two choices—blame him for my future failures or pick myself up, get a job, and grind. I started bagging groceries at age 14 and I haven't stopped working since. I love winning, but I also fear losing everything based on my family experience. That's part of what drives me—fear of failure and someone taking something from me and my family.

I planned on finishing my college degree in the fall of 1997, but my roommate convinced me we should move to Seattle in the fall instead. With his help, I figured out how to take four classes during the preceding summer semester and graduate before our departure. We planned to spend six months in Seattle, but ended up in the San Francisco Bay Area. I never left. I was desperate to pay rent because eviction meant someone taking something from me. That also meant I was always on the lookout for the next best job. In seven short years, I bounced between five companies, taking jobs as a corporate recruiter, a finance trainee, an advertising sales guy, and as an entry-level sales rep in the software industry, which is how my career really got started. One day a friend asked me to take a meeting with a sales manager at the multinational data storage company EMC. Next thing I knew, I was in front of the head of EMC's North American sales. He looked me in the eye and said, "Your career is a mess. Come build a career with EMC." So that's what I did.

EMC was an amazing place to train and succeed as a young person, selling enterprise hardware and software solutions. I spent eight years there, working for the same boss the entire time and ascending to the position of district sales manager for Northern California. He taught me the fundamentals of selling and how to lead sales teams. His mantra was to recruit and develop great people, and to drive revenue. He was great at the sales journey—understanding a customer's decision process, identifying champions within an account, and discovering the customer pain that EMC solutions could help alleviate. But I realized I did not want my boss's job. I needed to make a career change.

I had a number of job offers but I chose the security software startup Aveksa. They hired me as vice president of sales for the West Coast. The product was a hard sale but I loved the challenge. Unfortunately, that challenge didn't last long. About a year later, EMC acquired Aveksa. My heart sank. I did well at EMC and learned a ton about selling but I didn't want to go back. I realized that I needed to be passionate about what I sell. I'm a lousy liar, to be honest. If I don't love what I sell then people will see that from a mile away. I was convinced EMC had missed the boat by investing in hardware for on-premises data storage. In Silicon Valley, the data storage industry was heading to the cloud, however long it took to get there.

During my search for a new opportunity, a mutual business contact connected me with Mike Speiser. He was, and still is, a venture capitalist for Sutter Hill in Silicon Valley. Mike is fairly unique. He often bypasses the typical VC approach of waiting for software engineers to come up with new product ideas and then provide them with initial funding. Instead, he envisions a solution that could disrupt a sector of the tech industry and elicits input from experts to hone a product road map. That's how Snowflake was born. Mike pitched a raw idea to Benoit Dageville, who is a world-class database architect but was languishing at Oracle, plugging holes in its decades-old legacy database product. Benoit recommended a somewhat different approach and introduced Mike to his good friend and fellow Oracle database architect, Thierry Cruanes. Soon after, they started Snowflake in August 2012. Marcin Zukowski joined five months later as a co-founder. He was an expert in vector computing, which would become integral to Snowflake's product strategy.

Mike helped in a big way to assemble the first group of Snowflake engineers who would spend their days whiteboarding the product architecture and coding software. He was also the company's interim CEO, working one day a week in our tiny office and establishing a great working relationship with the team. The engineers often teased Mike for telling them: "Type faster. You guys need to type faster!" But selling Benoit and Thierry on hiring someone like me took some effort. It was November 2013 and Snowflake had 12 employees, including an office admin, who established Snowflake's office culture early on. The engineers didn't see a need for someone like me this soon at the company. A product-ready version of Snowflake for customers was still two years away. But Mike was keen to embed a salesperson to help the engineers. Sounds like an odd match—hiring for two areas of a company that couldn't be any further from each other in terms of the entire product chain.

The reluctance inside of Snowflake to hire me paled in comparison to my own trepidation. By day two at the company I thought, "Holy crap! What have I done?" I was in this small office in downtown San Mateo, California, with a small team of engineers. I spent a lot of time in a conference room with some knowledge about a product that didn't exist yet. I started cold calling. I thought the walls were somewhat soundproof but I could hear the engineers laughing. I found out later that 90 percent of what I first said about the technology was wrong. But that didn't matter. I was working with humble people who were aspiring to build something great.

Hire a Head of Sales While You're Still in Stealth

Mike Speiser basically forced the engineers to hire me. He wanted customer feedback while Snowflake was still in stealth mode—the period when the software engineers were building the product. Mike believed that if you're going after a huge market you have to nail the product market fit. That doesn't happen by sticking to your initial product development plan all the way to general availability (GA), hoping you will then sign a bunch of customers. We wanted to find out what architectural elements and product features Snowflake needed while our engineers were still pounding out software code. I started pitching to prospects what we had planned for the first public release of Snowflake. After that, but before GA, we had a beta version that prospects could trial. We gained a ton of feedback, so the list of desired features kept growing. Our engineers had to make architectural changes because Snowflake wasn't scaling well even though we were building it for the cloud. There was a lot of valuable customer feedback that took months to incorporate during stealth mode.

Choose Wisely

Your founders and founding engineers are your first product managers and marketers. They make all product decisions based on initial feedback from the market. That also means they often prefer a product manager or product marketer to lead sales and someone similar to lead marketing. Don't let this happen. Product managers determine which features and functionality the product will include. They likely have a degree in computer science or mathematics but never spent much time as a software engineer. Product marketers have some level of technical know-how, so they're great at explaining the technical features of your solution. But they're not so great at revealing a customer's business pain points such as declining revenue, profits, and efficiencies, and how your product can help reverse those trends. Those conversations will surely emerge as you move horizontally and hierarchically through all of the purchase influencers at a prospective customer. Even moving up a customer's engineering organization, those vice presidents want to hear about increasing engineering productivity, while reducing risk and time to market. They don't want to hear about new features. That's four levels down in their organizations. Moreover, product managers and product marketers have zero experience generating demand, which is critical to generating interest and feedback during your product's development phase and then capitalizing on those relationships when your product is available for sale.

At the same time, avoid hiring the relationship-only sales professional. These are seasoned sales folks who are more band leaders, when what a startup needs is a one-person band. They orchestrate and rely on a group of colleagues to conduct the sales motion. They include pre-sales engineers to meet with a customer's technical buyers, industry experts who know a customer's specific pain points, and professional services people who can understand a customer's existing computing environment and recommend training for technical and business users. They may also recommend a third-party service provider that offers necessary integration and implementation services your company doesn't offer. All of these roles are important when positioning and selling a technology but they don't yet exist at a startup. Without them, a pure relationship salesperson will fail.

Instead, strike a balance between the two. Your head of sales, your very first sales hire, should be someone who has a proven track record but not decades of experience. They have to roll up their sleeves in the beginning but then hire and lead a small but driven sales organization in the near future. They have to start from ground zero, make cold calls all day long, and get used to prospects saying "No thanks," or just hanging up on them. In essence, they have to be hungry and smart.

They must also have the aptitude and curiosity to understand technology as a layperson. They will face a room full of technical and business buyers when delivering a product presentation on their own and have to know what they're talking about. They may not know the answer to every product question a customer has but they should understand the question enough to later convey it clearly and completely to your engineers. And when your head of sales does get the answer, they must understand it just as well, or better, than they did the question. They should also take the time to learn about your product even when there is no product training or documentation available. If they can answer the majority of a customer's questions on the spot, that builds credibility and accelerates the sales cycle. It shows organizations that the person you've hired to lead this part of your company in the early stages is not just some go-between.

A Head of Sales Can Precede Your CEO

Bob Muglia joined as Snowflake's first full-time CEO seven months after I arrived. But Bob wasn't a CEO who had prior experience running sales organizations. And you wouldn't expect that from most CEOs of early-stage companies. Startups that last and experience hypergrowth during their first 10 years should see two or more successive CEOs with very different backgrounds to ensure an organization's success. On the flip side, I had some sales experience at a startup, and the only managerial position I occupied for a decent amount of time was district sales manager at EMC. All told, I had just over 12 years of sales experience. When I arrived, I still needed advice on how to be successful at a small software company and how to grow Snowflake's sales as the business transformed every few months.

Your Board Must Have Depth

A lot of executives are lonely. It can be a very isolating experience when you are responsible for a function, a department, or a geographic region for a company. And that's especially true if you are in marketing and your CEO is not a marketing expert. Or, you're in sales, and your CEO has little or no experience managing a sales organization. You need the opportunity to turn to others in your field for input and guidance. Getting advice from operational experts on the board who had been through the kind of hypergrowth we've had over the years at Snowflake was critical.

One of the conditions I put to Mike Speiser before agreeing to come to Snowflake was that I needed someone on the board who knows and respects sales. "Like who?" Mike asked. My response was "How about a guy like John McMahon?" I knew John from my time at Aveksa. He was one of the best sales executives in the industry and went on to write the highly successful book, *The Qualified Sales Leader*. Mike put John on Snowflake's board the next day. Getting board members who have been successful operators is vital. Even Mike is a former operator himself and he picked the Snowflake board very carefully.

This was the first time I was head of sales, anywhere, and my time at EMC involved selling hardware more than software. I met with different customers with different personas and encountered different use cases. The pricing was different, too. Snowflake was not only a software-as-a-service but one of the first tech companies to offer consumption-based pricing instead of subscription pricing. John was someone I could exchange ideas with. At board meetings, he could translate for me what was being said and he was usually right.

John had operated at a much higher level than me, as well. He helped me create the ideal customer profile and ideal salesperson profile, and explained he showed how to scale the sales organization as we started to grow. And he was constantly checking our productivity metrics to ensure we were growing fast enough but not getting ahead of ourselves. He was incredibly useful in letting me know how I was doing and anticipating problems that would emerge down the road, as the company grew its revenue and increased its number and types of customers. He was always asking, "What are the next steps?" John coached me on what I was seeing in real time. He also suggested what I would have to put in place if Snowflake took off, which it did. These were things I wouldn't know about, yet he had seen them many times before. "If you wait, it's almost too late, and then you're slowing everything down," John once said to me. Even if it was a pitch down the middle of the plate, I might not have seen a ball moving that fast before.

When Bob joined as CEO, he relied on John to help build and evolve the sales organization. There can be a lot of tension between finance and sales as you scale, because it's expensive to build an enterprise sales team. John would tell Bob, "Here's the model and here's what you do." So when Bob would question me, or when finance and I disagreed over costs, John would be the tiebreaker a lot of times. His input was incredibly helpful, helping to guide me and educating leadership about how to build, run, and transition a sales organization.

Having engaged and experienced board members, who have run organizations in specific domains and can mentor your startup's executives, is crucial to your success. Denise Persson had already been head of marketing at two companies for more than 10 years before she arrived at Snowflake in 2016. But she too sought out advice from another Snowflake board member. Jeremy Burton had been the CMO at Symantec, EMC, and Dell. He had also been a senior vice president of marketing at Oracle. Jeremy and Denise would exchange ideas and confirm what she was telling the board, or he would challenge her on ideas that he may not have agreed with. She also has a network of CMOs at other larger companies who had dealt with issues around company branding and messaging, demand generation, and hiring executives who would report to her. You need a network of seasoned executives who you can talk to confidentially. You have to be motivated to learn every day from colleagues and leaders, and from videos, books, journals, webinars, and podcasts. The minute that you think you know enough, you are lost.

Since those early days, Denise and I have consulted to a number of boards of software companies. Venture capitalists and others who sit on boards can't be generalists. They must be domain experts. Otherwise, they don't know how to guide executives or steer companies toward success. Generalists don't have operational experience, they don't have the backbone to make decisions, and they often regurgitate what they hear from other boards. Nothing beats an operator who gives great feedback.

Choose Receptive Executives

On the other side of this equation, your executives, at every stage of the company, must be coachable. Many aren't. It's nice to have an adult in the room who can give advice. Your head of sales, marketing, and all other functions must be motivated by constant learning. As an advisor, when I tell executives to do something, they often don't listen. I'm not just giving my advice. It's advice that's been handed down from generations of seasoned executives who have succeeded, and more importantly, who have failed and then gone on to succeed. It's advice that's been tried, scrutinized, and enhanced. If you do not listen to people who have done this before, you will fail. And your execs must also take hard feedback constructively, not personally. They have to see the value in the advice, act on it, and always remain adaptable. I'm absolutely sure that if I wasn't coachable and adaptable

I wouldn't have been tapped to become Snowflake's CRO. Early on, the board planned to eventually hire someone above me to lead sales but didn't. In one way or another, I occupied that role for more than 11 years.

This is especially important for young entrepreneurs. A brilliant software engineer with a disruptive approach to an existing technology sector can be priceless. But brains and ingenuity aren't replacements for experience. This couldn't be more true for the technology industry, where it's not uncommon for a 20-something engineer with a PhD to start a software company. The company's department heads will need an immense amount of guidance from board members who are seasoned operators in sales, marketing, finance, and a host of other areas. They will also need help building and running an engineering organization.

Above all else, founders should focus on their core expertise. Most want to do everything. They want to be CEO. Then they fail, and they make so many mistakes that they drag everyone else down. What got me excited about Snowflake was that our founders were passionate without attitude. In Silicon Valley, there are a lot of extremely large egos. Benoit and Thierry just wanted to solve problems. They are very smart and very human. But they let the rest of us figure out the go-to-market strategy for Snowflake's product.

Align Sales with Engineering

I had to build trust immediately with the engineers. In a larger organization, there are a number of teams between engineers and sales reps. They include product management, product marketing, and pre-sales engineering. None of them existed when I arrived in 2013. I was it. But I saw it as an opportunity to establish relationships with these really smart people with PhDs in building databases. At its core, Snowflake is an amazing database but much more.

Engineers are in a different stratosphere in terms of brainpower and specialized knowledge. All they really care about is making an awesome product that makes customers super happy. They had the ideas but they wanted to hear what customers needed. I had sold other solutions so that made me proficient, not fluent, in their language.

That's about as much as someone without an education or experience in coding software can offer. That's what I brought to the table. They figured me out pretty quickly and explained the product from that perspective. In parallel, they spoke from a competitive context—how other products were built, what were their benefits and flaws, and how Snowflake's architecture and features would serve customers better in the world of "big data" back then.

These men and women also had a sense of humor. It wasn't all code to them, all the time. Abdul Munir is one of the founding engineers at Snowflake. He would jokingly call me our "shadow CTO," because there was never a moment that I dictated anything from a product direction perspective. But I would influence that. I brought back input from prospective customers before our product was commercially available. If we incorporated what they wanted, then customers would buy Snowflake. I held myself accountable to that.

Software engineers can be incredibly focused and their time is often limited. In the early startup stage, they represent the vast majority of employees. That makes them the only product resource for sales. Make connections with them early on, and deliver as much value to them as you request of them. It will establish the beginnings of a solid company culture and serve both organizations well in later years even as other teams emerge as conduits between engineering and sales. Having an engineer engage a prospective customer every so often can have an immense impact. Technical decision-makers are often the first people at a customer that you have to win over. In the early days of your company, or down the road, connecting one of your engineers with a key technical buyer can help unstick a deal and move that customer faster through the sales cycle.

Jump-Start Your Company Culture

What does culture look like with a company of less than 20 people? It's there, but it's in the background. Everyone is working long hours toward a common goal that is years away—developing a customer-ready product that organizations need. That could easily obscure the need to reveal and live a company culture. Don't let it. Even the simplest things in those early days can shape what a company's culture will become. Startups come and go, and those who sign up to work for one know that. On a whiteboard, Snowflake looked as though it could be something great but none of us knew for sure. During my entire time at Snowflake, I always said I was on a three-month contract, not knowing what the future held for any of us. In those early days, having a culture, no matter how pervasive, helped instill in us that we were a humble team that would succeed or fail together.

Nancy Venezia arrived six months before me. She was Snowflake's office manager and employee number eight. She handled purchasing, payroll, and any immigration action items as she onboarded new employees. Most importantly, she was the glue that held everyone together in those early years. "We were all very close. It wasn't a family you came home to but it was our work family," Nancy once said. "So, I wanted people to fall in love with Snowflake the way I did. I wanted them to know they weren't just working for a great company. I wanted them to know they were working with great people."

Every employee and every candidate for hire had to pass by Nancy when they entered Snowflake's small office space. She got to know them all. No one who ended up working at Snowflake had an ego, including those who held senior positions at previous companies. Nancy saw that as an opportunity to start bringing everyone together to foster what would become Snowflake's culture and the company's values that followed.

We ordered lunch into the office every day of the week but one. On those days, we all crammed into "The Lodge," the largest space in the office that was our kitchen and our biggest meeting space. We were all so busy but we carved out 30 minutes of each day to sit with each other and share a meal. It didn't matter which team you worked for, what language was your first language, or how long you had been at Snowflake. It was a lively time as we all got to know a lot about each other and shared what we were working on.

Once a year, and just before Thanksgiving, Nancy organized an international potluck. She encouraged employees to bring a dish that represented their culture. Even as a small company, we hailed from at least half a dozen countries. She wanted everyone to feel that they belonged. She also organized Fruity Fridays and a costume contest on every Halloween.

She created Waffle Wednesdays, for which the engineers happily cooked every week. And it wasn't just waffles. They went all out to prepare a great breakfast. Even after we moved to our second office space, the tradition continued with our techies donning aprons to feed more than 100 employees. Nancy also created Cheesy Thursday, which happened once a month. We gathered for a drink and cheese and crackers in the late afternoon. Nancy departed Snowflake in 2019. We moved our Silicon Valley offices more than once to accommodate our growth, but Waffle Wednesdays still happen thanks to Nancy's legacy and our cafeteria staff.

The biggest event, which started just prior to Nancy's arrival, was the annual Snowflake ski trip. Our founders chose "Snowflake" as the company name for a number of reasons, which included their love of skiing. There's still a photo somewhere in the office of the first five employees at NorthStar ski resort in Lake Tahoe in 2013. That trip continued for a few more years until it was no longer feasible. But when it did happen, Nancy was in the middle of it, making sure we all had a memorable experience.

In the early days of a company, there isn't much structure but there's plenty of uncertainty. Addressing both of those issues is possible with simple experiences that bring employees together. In those first few years, we had almost no attrition. We were voted one of the best places to work, year after year. And this evolving and inclusive culture paved the way to Snowflake developing its company values that we still live by every day. Make events like these a must in any small company. If you don't have an office manager, get one. Or, distribute event planning to your most eager employees who have the free time.

2

Develop Your Sales Strategy

"In those early days, we were intellectually honest with ourselves about what the product could do and how to sell it."

—Chris Degnan

SNOWFLAKE WAS BUILT to do many things with data. One of those is data warehousing—a sector of the technology industry that emerged more than 20 years before Snowflake's founders typed their first line of code. It was ripe for disruption, so they got working on a solution that was vastly different from our competitors' legacy technology.

By the 1980s, companies were becoming more aware of the analytical insights trapped inside their databases designed solely for online transaction processing (OLTP). These solutions handled thousands of small data entries to add, update, and delete information each day. It all came from an organization's sales, marketing, payroll, invoicing, purchasing, and inventory management teams, to name just a few. But when they attempted to analyze this information for business planning, their OLTP databases would slow or even crash. The analytical power needed pushed these systems beyond their limits.

At the time, the only way to get around this problem was to copy that data into a different type of database for analysis only. Hence, the online analytical processing (OLAP) database, or data warehouse, was born. Instead of millions of small updates to the data in OLTP systems, data warehouses were designed to handle incredibly large queries of the data in the warehouse. The insights derived from that data informed every part of a business, revealed previously unforeseen efficiencies, and brought into view new market opportunities.

These data warehouses were often at the core of an organization's data strategy, yet their own limitations emerged not long after their creation. They couldn't scale to keep pace with the vast amount of data available beyond what organizations created on their own. The explosion of data from website traffic, smartphone usage, and IoT (Internet of Things) sensors created exponentially more data, kicking off the era of "big data" at the start of this century. Modern forms of data sharing, app development, and unifying data silos have continued this trend and fuel data-hungry pursuits such as artificial intelligence (AI), machine learning (ML), and generative AI.

Determine What Differentiates Your Product

The first thing you must determine are the major features your product offers over your competitors' and what problems they solve for customers. I talked at length with our founders and first engineers about what made Snowflake different. Back then I was still wrestling with how to message to customers the benefits of Snowflake's data warehouse. Benoit and Thierry knew the product was cool but explaining it to a layperson like me, who then had to message it to customers, had its challenges. They would end up getting into the technical weeds of Snowflake. "I don't understand what you're saying," I told them. "Dumb it down for me so that I can explain it." And that's what they did.

I learned how Snowflake's data warehouse architecturally separated data storage from the computing horsepower needed to analyze all of that data. This was a first in the industry. Other products coupled the two elements together on the same disk. The idea back then was that close proximity between the two elements meant better performance. But the downsides of this approach were many, such as limiting an organization's ability to increase data storage and computing independently of each other.

And similar to legacy on-premises data warehouses, Snowflake could ingest structured data, which is stored in tables as numbers, dates, and short text. MS Excel is a form of structured data. But traditional data warehouses could not store semi-structured data, which does not have the rigid format of structured data. This type of data became more common and included the JavaScript Object Notation (JSON) format. Semi-structured JSON data could be data from IoT devices, web browsing activity, and smartphone usage. To capture this vital information, organizations had to store it in Hadoop, which was not a data warehouse but an open framework that comprised a number of different modules of that solution. By the 2010s, Hadoop was good at storing this type of data but difficult at extracting and analyzing it. In essence, Snowflake was able to store and analyze both structured and semi-structured data, consolidating the benefits of two products—the legacy data warehouse and Hadoop—into just one solution.

Snowflake was also the first data warehouse built to operate solely for the cloud. All other solutions were built for each customer's hardware that they housed and managed on their own premises. This forced customers to buy way more hardware than they first needed, knowing they would eventually need more later as their data needs increased. Until then, they would have to own and manage idle hardware because the complex challenge of adding hardware to an existing system would make it near impossible. Worse off, the day would come when they would exceed their hardware constraints, forcing them to copy data to other repositories for data analysis. The result was data sprawl—a data governance nightmare. Customers would also have to run non-essential data activities at night and on weekends to avoid slower response times when business users analyzed data during normal business hours. In the cloud, with a product built for the cloud, there is nearly endless data storage and computing power available. A customer could dedicate any amount of computing power to each data workload and dial down that computing once a job completed. All the while, all of those workloads were simultaneously accessing a single copy of the data. These and other unique architectural differences made Snowflake much more powerful and much easier to use versus teams of hardware and software professionals required to babysit an on-premises solution. Snowflake took care of all that management with a cloud-built data warehouse as a service.

So, that's what we focused on in the early days: storage separate from computing, natively ingesting semi-structured data, the limitless power of the cloud, and near-zero management required by the customer. Those core architectural features were the background of our messaging and what I used to build my sales pitch.

Your startup likely began the same way, or it should. Your founders had been analyzing an area of industry during their undergraduate or postgraduate studies and determined a gap or need in the market for a technology the incumbents didn't offer. Others worked for one or a number of similar technology companies and figured out they could build a product that was architecturally superior and offered enough new features that would significantly differentiate their solution from the major market players. On the flip side, the tech industry has always been littered with "solutions" that offer something new but very little in the way of value. "A lot of times developers think they have a new platform or an app, when what they've developed is just a feature," Bob Muglia once told me. When that happens, the more probable path for success is to sell that feature to the company of the app for which it was originally designed to enhance.

Keep It Simple, for Now

As Snowflake's product development progressed, our own team realized that what they were building was more than a product that would disrupt the data warehouse market. "We were developing a platform," one of our founding engineers, Ashish Motivala, once told me.

A true computing platform is pretty huge. It has many use cases, and data warehousing could be just one of them. It's also not just a product you use but one that you can build your own software products with to use internally or offer commercially. This would be transformative for customers, and that enticed me. What could Snowflake become one day? The next Microsoft or Oracle? But those lofty pursuits would have to wait. We were a tiny group with a promising technology that would offer benefits other data warehouses didn't. At the same time, it would lack bread-and-butter features that competitors' products had been offering for years.

Wholeheartedly diving into the abyss of positioning Snowflake as a platform crossed my mind. Yet, I knew better. I had 10 years of sales experience, most of which I acquired at EMC. If you want to grow big, you have to keep it simple and focus small. We stuck with cloud data warehousing and it worked. Not just then but even 3 years down the road when Denise arrived. I remember a meeting of the executive team and a few others around that time. I told them: "Data warehouse. That has to be in the product name. When it comes to IT spending, customers have a budget line item that says 'data warehouse.'" For me, there was no clearer justification to offer a product that appeared so prominently in a customer's IT strategy. My input came in response to a months-long branding exercise that Denise understandably kicked off with an independent firm in Silicon Valley. It could have changed "data warehouse" to something else, including "data platform." That exercise was exhaustive and delivered a huge insight to our marketing and sales organizations. It also revealed we should stick with "data warehouse," for now.

Develop Your Ideal Customer Profile

Armed with our product's unique benefits, we went to work to develop our ideal customer profile (ICP). I worked with John McMahon on Snowflake's initial ICP. According to John, you have to answer the following questions to determine that profile:

What are the major differentiators in my product?

What pain points does the product solve for the customer?

Inside of which use cases do those pain points emerge?

Who (which personas) owns those use cases?

In which companies are those personas and use cases located?

Based on this information, John and I started with a very narrow profile—technical professionals working for ad tech companies and gaming companies with fewer than 1,000 employees. Ad tech platforms serve up millions of ads per second. Whenever you go to a website, 10 ads pop up and 10 JSON files are created, for example. Multiply that by tens of millions of users and you get trillions of JSON files.

For online gaming, every time you pulled the virtual slot machine, a JSON file was created. While you're playing, dozens of JSON files are created based on what you're looking at, what actions you took, and how long you've been playing the game. If the game is popular, those microtransactions generate astronomical amounts of JSON data. And online gaming and ad tech were already in the cloud. On-premises computer servers didn't have the capacity to handle that volume.

Armed with that information, we targeted tech professionals such as database administrators, whose jobs were to keep on-premises data warehouses up and running. We also sought out data engineers, who were in charge of the data pipeline. They develop methods to locate, move, and convert raw data into information data analysts and data scientists can use to extract insights. Snowflake was still in beta back then, and even when the product became generally available, we mainly sold to personas in these two industries. The total addressable market for data warehousing back then was $10 billion but we focused on a small part of that. "What we have to do is keep going down these two bowling alleys," John told me. "As much as we can, sell to those ad tech and gaming companies and keep giving feedback to Thierry and Benoit. As they expand the product, you'll be able to go down another bowling alley, and another. But you have to have patience."

John was right. Even when I sold into ad tech and gaming, I spent small amounts of time gathering data from other industries and companies of other sizes. I wanted the engineers to know the new features and functionalities we had to add so we could eventually expand our ICP. I was finding product market fit through sales, not marketing, because that function didn't yet exist at Snowflake, and not engineering because those guys needed to focus on developing the product.

Develop Your Sales Pitch

The benefits of Snowflake over our competitors' products were obvious to us, of course. But our company and our product were unknowns to everyone who knew the database, data warehouse, and especially the data platform sectors of the tech industry. So, we carried forward what our founders and engineers started—solving customers' problems. Snowflake's unique architecture and initial set of features defined us, but leading with that message would be akin to the young shepherd David attempting to sling a stone the size of a Chevy at his much larger adversary.

Instead, we positioned at the forefront of our messaging the issues that forced our targeted personas to waste vast amounts of time on laborious tasks—tasks that were necessary and preliminary steps before they could actually analyze data to reveal and address their business problems. We took the view that there was no sense selling someone a car that had air-conditioned seats and power sunroofs but required them to tune the engine every day in order to keep it moving.

I had to find the wording that would get customers interested. For our zero-management pitch, I explained to customers that the 15 tasks they had to do, which would take them a weekend, we did it all automatically as a service. That was the iteration of the sales pitch. For example, data scientists had to do administrative tasks, such as "vacuum" their data warehouse and build sort keys and indexes. And they had to do this on weekends because weekdays were solely dedicated to performing analytics. If they attempted to perform vacuuming or other such tasks during the week, business users running queries on that data would see performance slow to a crawl or the system would crash altogether. All of a sudden, we changed that dynamic.

For harnessing the near limitless power of the cloud, we coined the phrase "multi-clustered shared data architecture" as the tagline to describe Snowflake's underlying architecture. Its name is a variation of the tagline to describe the legacy architecture our competitors' products were built upon. It used some of the same words, so we were talking their language but conveyed Snowflake was something much better. Each business and technical user who touched the data warehouse could access near-infinite amounts of dedicated computing power at their fingertips to execute their own data workloads, whenever and from wherever they wanted. There was no competing for computing power, and adding as many users as you wanted wouldn't impact performance. And there was only one copy of the data that they needed to access simultaneously.

But still, we positioned their issues at the forefront of our messaging. It's how most of us think as professionals—solve problems first. Then, and only then, did we back up our claims with our technology.

At some point, you need to flip the switch so customers stop rolling their eyes when they're hearing about features and functionality. Instead, tell them first the big problems you can solve for them that other products can't.

Generate Demand

I started at Snowflake in late 2013 and didn't hire my first sales rep until February 2014. Until then, I had to generate all customer demand on my own. A few months for a small startup with zero sales is a huge window of opportunity, or missed opportunity. I was at ground zero—a scary place and yet it propelled me to be the most resourceful and ingenious in my career up to that point. I signed up for our first Salesforce account and got to work.

Sutter Hill was still an immense resource for me to lean on and Mike Speiser was still interim CEO, working at our Snowflake office one day a week. Sutter Hill collected about 100 names of potential prospects before I arrived. The Snowflake folks let those prospects know what we were up to but they hadn't received much of a response. That list became the start of me manually building my own database of prospects. Our office manager, Nancy, was taking night classes and got to know a young college student who was looking for a part-time job. I hired her to help build lists. I would reach out to about 2,000 people a week. We would go to job boards and see who was posting jobs for our would-be competitors and we would contact those people. My goal was to generate eight meetings a week and I exceeded that on a regular basis. Then I would follow up with those prospects. I talked to them in their terms about how Snowflake could solve their data problems. To the contrary, speaking about features and functions is like throwing 100 puzzle pieces on a table and saying, "you figure it out." John McMahon convinced me that you have to put the pieces together so they can see what this picture is going to look like before they buy.

I had two major roles in the company when the product was pre-GA. I was a business development rep, making phone calls to get meetings with prospects and trying to get the product in front of prospects. The second part of my job was that of a product manager. I had to bring feedback from these prospects about the product to our engineers. I had to convey what they liked, what we could improve, and what they wanted in the product that was missing. Early on, it was a really tough job because the product was still being developed and we had nothing to sell. I would make my own lists, send my own emails, make cold calls, and then get in front of prospects. I would then give that feedback to the engineers and founders so they could further develop the product. I asked prospects to prioritize three to five must-have features they would like to see added to the product. Often, I would get a prospect on the phone with Benoit and Thierry to explain what they wanted. Once a company grows, you have product managers who do that but we weren't there yet.

Of special note, there was one aspect of Snowflake sales in those early days that I didn't see coming. The data warehouse industry had been established decades before I started pitching to customers. Those legacy systems were built to operate solely in on-premises computing environments and they were dinosaurs by then. Snowflake only operated in the cloud and the architecture our founders and engineers designed and built had never been attempted. When I did get in front of prospects, they flat out didn't believe what I was peddling was possible. I would say more often than not: "Don't believe anything I say. Assume I'm a liar and try it out because you are not going to believe it." It didn't end there. After we went GA, and customers did buy the product, they attempted to operate it similar to the legacy on-premises system that we replaced. They had no other such experience with a data warehouse up until Snowflake. In essence, they were still trying to drive a 1972 Buick, when we just sold them a car that could fly.

Be a Product Manager, Not a Product Monster

Selling successfully at an early-stage startup has a few major components. Developing a growing pipeline of qualified leads is one of them. Being a good product manager is another. Convincing engineers which new features they should add based on customer feedback is a no-no. The list of product features customers want added to your product will never end. And that list will only grow as your product management and engineering teams grow. A sales leader of a startup will be tempted to push certain desired features over others, thinking those features will help close a quick deal. Don't let that happen. At this stage, engineers are best to prioritize this list. They know what the product is missing and which new features will have the biggest impact across the largest number of potential customers. Those features must happen first. Niche or nice-to-have features will come later, even if it means your company won't land a Fortune 500 customer until they do. A sales leader who attempts to influence that process will only sour their relationship with their engineers. When it comes to personalities, there's not much common ground between the two and sales folks are the ones more likely to irk engineers—not the other way around.

Related to this, your pre- and post-GA product will be missing a whole bunch of features that your competitors' products have offered for years. That's okay. Those bread-and-butter features are not why your product first exists. Instead, your founders and your first engineers set out to disrupt an industry, not emulate it. They determined that what was on offer before they arrived failed to solve a multitude of customers' problems, which stifled their ability to grow their businesses. Snowflake was conceived on such a premise. Our product's architecture was revolutionary. To this day, it remains the bedrock of how we continue to add amazing new features to the product. But focusing on building something so new from scratch had its tradeoffs. Our product lacked basic features, such as data loading, data security, and data deduplication. What we could offer in the beginning overshadowed the features that prospects expected Snowflake to have but came later. What our founders and engineers developed from the outset, which comprised my initial sales pitch, created enough customer appeal to get them interested, provide me product feedback, and eventually generate a constant and growing revenue stream.

Be Patient, Remain Focused, and Be Humble

While this was happening, I realized the importance of having someone like me in this job. As I mentioned in Chapter 1, hiring a head of sales early on with the right amount of experience is key. I didn't mind going it alone for a while and doing some tasks that a recent college grad could handle. Sales reps often do. Sure, they have managers and technical sales consultants who often help out. But most of the time we're on our own and we're wholly responsible for making our quota no matter what the stated goals are in our annual contracts. Rarely do companies these days overpopulate a region or industry with too many of their sales reps. There are many software tools that help automate the process of accurately revealing the potential viability of a sales region. From there, you choose the annual quotas and the number of reps to match that viability. If a sales rep repeatedly falls short of their quota, they're likely in the wrong job. I set my goals early on and exceeded them. If I failed, the Snowflake board had every right to fire me. I never gave them a reason to and no one else did either.

In those early days, the engineers were available when I needed to meet with them so I could develop my sales pitch, and they were very receptive to hearing the product feedback I received from prospects. John McMahon and I met on a regular basis and he bestowed upon me his vast knowledge about sales. When a sales rep falls short, that person's customers and prospects are not getting the knowledge and value they need to make the best business decisions or best technology decisions, respectively speaking. The company suffers because it's giving up customers and revenue to competitors that may not necessarily have a superior product. If I failed, an entire company could fall over, or at least be no closer to the revenue we desperately needed to help get us from one financial quarter to the next. Venture capital funding is not a money tree. In essence, I had to be focused, and be at least as good at sales as our engineers were at developing the product. And those people are pretty amazing.

If you're not prone to being humble, start. It's what has kept Snowflake grounded. Silicon Valley is full of super egos, and justifiably so. There's an incredible amount of very smart, skilled, and talented people here. Without humbleness in that mix, it can become pure arrogance. Decades ago the Valley was lauded for that type of behavior, from executive leadership all the way down to newly hired college grads. People would foster or become victims of brutal work environments. Not only would morale suffer but so would the customer experience and company performance. Some of that still goes on today. Snowflake's founders, our board, and our first engineers are all driven, accomplished, and humble people. I knew that from the outset and I emulated that as Snowflake's head of sales. It was particularly important that I do. The best sales managers and reps want to succeed. But they have to do so with respect for their customers and their colleagues. Otherwise, a sales team is just a bunch of lone cowgirls and cowboys shooting up the place. Read on to understand how we accomplished that.

3

Hiring and Deploying Your First Sales Reps

"You're someone who has a chip on your shoulder. ... Someone who questions everything."

—Kyle Rourke

KYLE WAS THE first sales rep I hired at Snowflake. We'd known each other for more than 10 years and we later worked together as peers at EMC. When I moved to Aveksa, I asked him to come work for me and run Aveksa sales for the Pacific Northwest. I called him again after I landed at Snowflake and hired him as head of sales for the West Coast. Kyle was employee number 35. I also hired Vince Trotta around the same time to run the east coast and one other field sales rep to handle the central US region. We too had a history before Snowflake. That was the core sales team for 2014. So, I started building a sales force around these first three leaders and I let them hire reps underneath them. By then, I had already hired two junior business development reps to help make cold calls.

Start with Who You Know

I can't stress this enough. The earlier the stage of a company the more crucial the hiring process. You not only need the best but you need people who are excited about your product and see your company as a great place to work. The investment you make with new hires is much higher early on. There are no systems in place and no training programs. So it was on me to personally get each new sales hire up to speed on the product and enticed with Snowflake—the company. All the while, I was still reaching out to thousands of prospects each week and scheduling my own meetings. An early departure from a small team is more likely to make colleagues rethink their plans versus someone leaving a company of hundreds, or thousands. One out of many is not the same as one out of five. It's also a downer for those who remain. Connections between coworkers go much deeper in small organizations. It's pure math. We spend more time with fewer people and rely on them more than in bigger organizations.

Success in my role from the outset was critical to Snowflake seeding the market early. I had big tech training and sales experience, did some time at a startup, and I wasn't too junior to jump-start a sales organization or too senior to roll up my sleeves. Mike Speiser hired me for my experience, and he trusted the person who recommended me. I deployed the same criticality when hiring Snowflake's first three field sales reps. They had the experience and proven track records of exceeding sales quotas. But people who make a career in technology sales are different from those who comprise the rest of the company. They must handle the constant pressure of meeting a quota, start from ground zero most days, and respond well to setbacks and defeat on a regular basis. That also means they can be unpredictable. Sales folks move from company to company more often than other professionals and even more so in software.

Established companies lose their edge and legacy products flatten out. Startups, and their allure of pre-IPO equity, come and go. New technologies emerge to challenge startups that are still in stealth mode. A single opportunity with an enterprise customer can involve 10 or more technology areas and a host of competitors vying for each slice of that pie. Any sales professional who is great at what they do is being tempted often by competitors and business partners to join them. But Kyle remained at Snowflake for 8 years in various sales and strategy leadership roles. Vince spent 10 years at the company, with the same career track as Kyle. I became the longest-serving founding CRO in the industry. This kind of longevity of the right people will help define a startup's future. A revolving door of early employees can limit it.

Seed, Don't Sell

The idea was to hire the people and get signals from the marketplace. None of us knew the data warehouse market, which turned out to be a benefit. We went in with fresh eyes and armed with a product that could upend the competition. We were still missing a thousand features but the team focused on the big picture. We sold $500 evaluation agreements for the first six to seven months in order to find all of the big deficiencies. We remained tight with the engineering team, which continued to grow faster than any other group in the company. In the beginning, none of the sales reps were on commission. I structured their compensation as salary plus additional payment for meeting a level of a predetermined set of MBOs, such as the number of qualified leads, customer meetings, and evaluation agreements that they generated.

In essence, I'm telling these reps that we have no customers, no website, and a product that isn't ready yet. There's no real market yet for a cloud data warehouse, because it's still all on-premises. "You're going to take a sizable pay cut to do this," I would tell them. And it's going to require a scorched-earth mentality to go find our own meetings, close our own deals, and you won't get a single dollar of commission to show for it. That's basically the sales pitch they got from me to join an early-stage startup. As Kyle once said: "I'm selling religion right now. Oh, and by the way, our biggest competitors will soon become Amazon Web Services, Microsoft, IBM, Dell, HP, and Teradata." Overall, sales is about recruiting, developing sales reps, and driving revenue. Those were the three things we focused on. If you recruit good people and you develop them, the rest will take care of itself.

Hire a Hiring Expert

I reached out to a sales recruiter, Chad Peets. He placed me at Aveksa and became a good friend. I thought about running sales recruitment within Snowflake but it just wasn't feasible. We became so busy with driving revenue that even searching for great candidates would have taken away from that, which we couldn't afford. "I'll find the candidates for you," he insisted. "You gotta let these guys drive the business. They can't afford to spend 30 hours a week on hiring."

Chad is energetic, to say the least. He and I collaborated on a process that resulted in the hiring of every Snowflake sales rep from 2015 up until the company went public in 2020—more than 500 people total. We had 15 reps in 2015, 30 in 2016, 100 in 2017, 300 in 2018, and so on. His interview-to-hire ratio was two to one. Chad once told me: "If you're going to scale something like that, it has to be an absolute machine." Nothing I'd seen had scaled so fast and so successfully. We continued to increase the size of the sales team with the benchmark of $1.5m of annual quota per rep once they were trained up and productive. We measured the heck out of the business to make sure we weren't hiring too fast.

Chad had a high bar for what made a good sales candidate for Snowflake. He interviewed everyone before he chose to pass them on to us. We didn't allow any negotiating over compensation packages. It just wasn't efficient. Chad was quick to uncover issues as the hiring process progressed. As multiple layers of management evolved in the sales organization, he detected some managers deviating from the hiring strategy and corrected that. The best interviews I had with potential sales leaders were people who put me on my heels and peppered me with questions, versus someone who hadn't researched the company and wasn't excited about what Snowflake was doing in the market. Chad brought us smart, experienced, and driven people who could see what the rest of us already knew.

Chad didn't always bring a ton of candidates but he brought great candidates. My job was to sell them on coming to a startup with a weird name that didn't have a product and didn't have much in the way of any revenue. But the hiring managers made the final decision. Once they did, Chad would call the person, make the offer, and only allow them to say "yes" or "no." If they asked for more money, Chad's response was always "no." "I speak on behalf of Chris Degnan. I don't need to check with him. The answer is 'no.'" We didn't have to manage going back and forth on salary. We wiped out all of the inefficiencies. Otherwise, you couldn't scale like we did. You would just run out of time.

The Sales Rep Profile: Gunslingers But Not Cowboys

We created an assessment that we had candidates fill out. It included about 100 questions and we asked the same question more than once. We were looking for the outliers. They had to be proactive, independent, and do things without being told. They could not be a slave to authority. The questions asked them to rate themselves between 1 and 10 on certain characteristics. We were looking for 1 (which was an absolute "no") on a lot of the questions that most hiring managers would consider a 10 (an absolute "yes") to be the best answer:

- **"Do you consider yourself an objective thinker?"** We wanted reps who go with their gut.
- **"Are you manageable?"** We searched for those who question everything.
- **"Do you do what you're told?"** Kyle was a "1." There were almost no resources available then to help train new sales reps. They had to be resourceful and find ways to learn about our technology and that of our competitors. We had no marketing team, so they had to find their own leads and write their own emails to prospects. If a rep needed to be told what to do in order to start selling Snowflake, they were at the wrong company.
- **Is having a chip on your shoulder bad?** We wanted that chip. The competition was out there. They were waiting to crush us, and prospects were ready to discard us. Our sales reps had to jettison any inhibitions that might creep up on them in the face of that eventuality. No matter their thoughts, they had to wake up every day with the mentality that no one was going to stop them from approaching the right prospects, getting a meeting with them, and pitching the Snowflake story.
- **Do you work well with others?** We wanted good people but a "1" was ideal. This was about self-reliance. We needed mavericks early on. If they believed they could handle anything on their own, they belonged at Snowflake. Sales opportunities move faster when fewer people are involved. If only one person has to engage a customer, all the better. That's rare in big sales organizations but it's necessary in a startup.

Do you need evidence to support your beliefs? We hoped not. We were selling religion before we actually had a product. And the religion we were selling was too good to be true. There was decades of evidence to show that what Snowflake promised, prospects wouldn't believe. When that happened, our reps had to properly convince them that what was coming with Snowflake was real and it would forever change how they managed and analyzed their data.

The assessment also included sections they had to complete on math and reading comprehension. If a candidate didn't get a certain score on the assessment, we decided they were not going to be a good fit for Snowflake at this stage of the company. If they made it to the interview stage, we would ask them to tell us about something difficult they'd been through in life. "What challenges have you faced?" "When you ran into an obstacle, what was it and how did you respond?" "Tell me one thing I should know about you." "Tell me where you went to elementary school." "What sports did you play in high school?"

We needed people who were more than just self-starters. We needed people who had a strong belief in themselves. They believed they were going to make themselves successful, versus relying on someone else for that. When you hire reps today, their first question is usually, "What kind of training am I going to get? I need a good engineer to work with. I need help understanding the product. I need all of these manuals and videos and webinars that big companies provide their sales reps." At a startup, there is no formalized training. Kyle made a training email with links to a bunch of stuff on YouTube. He would tell the new reps: "There you go, buddy. Go get it!" If you couldn't figure it out on your own, Snowflake probably wasn't going to work out for you.

Successful candidates had to be good at selling technology, but not necessarily at selling the relationship in those early days. They also had to be somewhat technical because we didn't have any pre-sales engineers who would normally handle the demo and address a customer's technical questions. Those folks were hired later. Sales reps had to be super smart, self-reliant, driven, coachable, somewhat pessimistic, and wanted the opportunity to be promoted to a second-tier or third-tier manager, with people working under them. That kind of rapid advancement doesn't happen at big established companies. Promotions and advancement take years. At Snowflake, you have to be someone who is eager to take control of your career and gain more responsibility quickly. We wanted hunters, not gatherers, who were willing to pick up the phone and cold call. And when confronted with a challenge, they didn't give up.

Sales professionals came to Snowflake because they wanted to be part of the growth of a startup that could become a major company. We didn't want people who had sold for large companies, landed the big whales, and were making three, four, or five hundred thousand dollars a year for a long time. A sales rep at Snowflake was not going to make that kind of money in those early years. Otherwise, they would quit in three months. We were closing $30,000 transactions back then. We hired young hungry people who had three to five years' experience and had experience turning prospects into customers. We made them productive very fast, so we could hire even faster.

These were gunslingers but not cowboys, especially in their personal lives. I was strong on ethics, morals, and values with the sales team in those early days. Sales is stressful and more so when mixed with the uncertain future of a startup. But that mix wasn't an excuse for bad behavior, on or off the field. Sales reps can be enormous partiers and get up to all kinds of mischief. At Snowflake, we couldn't afford that kind of behavior; nor could our customers. Eventually, as our sales force grew, and as we added more layers of management and more processes to train our reps, we altered the criteria of what made a great candidate for us. We didn't need an entire team of gunslingers.

Hiring from Competitors

We were open to hiring from our competitors to build our sales team. We used the same criteria as we did with non-competitive candidates. Yet, we chose not to hire sales reps who had worked for the legacy data warehouse providers. Those companies had begun porting their solutions to the cloud—an approach that didn't materially improve their product. It was less the technology and more the sales environments these reps had experienced that bothered us. They were often given an existing list of customers when they started their employment. That was the context of their sales efforts. The legacy data warehouse providers spent more time upgrading their existing clients than seeking out new ones. It made total sense. These technologies were already 20-plus years old by the time Snowflake made its product publicly available. This made their reps gatherers, not hunters, and we needed hunters.

But we did hire their top pre-sales engineers who were successful in that environment and keen to work for Snowflake. The engineers didn't have to hunt, really. In almost every software company, they are paired with at least one sales rep to conduct the technical side of the sale. Deals don't close without their time spent with a customer's technical decision-makers. And coming from the legacy world, those sales engineers knew how to approach large organizations that had been relying on this technology and showed them how Snowflake could alleviate what they endured for years thanks to those aging technologies. They also became crucial once our marketing team arrived. Those sales engineers were critical to the development of our competitive migration guides, which marketing created until we established a formidable professional services organization. We also hired very competent people as sales engineers who worked for tech companies that weren't our competitors.

Lead By Example

I was still going on my own sales calls as we began to hire, so I held my team to the same accountability. Any sales rep who worked for me had to go to eight face-to-face meetings each week. I would send a weekly email to the entire company that detailed my own sales efforts: "I had this amount of customer meetings, here's who I met with, and this is what they're looking for in a data warehouse." I also sent a win wire each week to the entire company. Every deal was a win and it was incredibly helpful. Everyone loved learning about the companies we were talking to, what each deal was about, and how we won the business.

I had to lead by example, because at this stage, it was crucial to build trust and awareness. As a startup, the fear is that the technology won't work and your customer champion gets fired. After the purchase, you can still disappoint the customer. Now you're less competitive. It was more a partnership with our first paying customers. We couldn't jeopardize their success. If we did, we would jeopardize ours. We didn't sign up customers to multi-year deals because we couldn't get anyone to commit to such a contract while the product was still so new.

Minnows, Not Whales

John McMahon warned me early on: "When you're the size of a startup, where you have very little revenue, you don't want to hook up with a big customer, because then you got a tiger by the tail. They give you a huge order and then they own you. And then you feel like you have to deliver on whatever they ask for. It could take your product and your company in a direction you just don't want to go. Many startups have made that mistake and it killed them."

We didn't recruit whale hunters (enterprise sales reps) because we didn't have the resources if we hooked a whale. Once you start selling to large accounts, all of the product requirements grow—data security requirements, new feature demands, and integration with their existing environments. We were short on all of that in the beginning. The most common mistake startup founders make is they want to go after big accounts too soon. Instead of continuing on the path of product development to serve your current market and expand into other markets, your engineers become order takers. Worse off, it's likely that what they're developing for that one whale isn't something that will benefit other customers, or enough customers in order to justify incorporating that functionality sooner rather than later. As mentioned previously, Snowflake's founders and engineers were driven to solve customers' problems. They still are. But their success depended on a manageable process to address those problems. Otherwise, you could turn your engineers into an angry mob and understandably so.

This also meant we focused on cloud-native customers. Back then, it was likely that newer companies built their businesses on a cloud-only strategy. The shift from on-premises computing to cloud was in its early stage but the benefits were clear. And it was obvious how much work large established companies had ahead of them to slowly migrate to the cloud over a number of years. It was similar to the old adage of turning an aircraft carrier in the opposite direction. We sold customers on Snowflake's cloud data warehouse. We didn't sell them on the cloud. They had to already be in the cloud, or at least believe in the cloud, before we arrived.

John McMahon and I spent a lot of time discussing what constituted an "A" opportunity for Snowflake at the time, versus what was a "B" or "C" opportunity. He wanted me to focus on the "A" customers in ad tech and online gaming. "B" and "C" opportunities were companies in financial services, healthcare, and retail. Those enterprises had to comply with payment card industry (PCI) and HIPAA requirements. Data encryption and connecting to business intelligence (BI) and extract, transform and load (ETL) tools were also features we didn't support yet. An "A" opportunity to Snowflake back then had none of those requirements but would have been a "C" opportunity to one of our much larger and more established competitors. And the opposite was true for what we considered to be a "C" opportunity.

There's still a famous quote that's heard around Snowflake from a customer meeting we had with a Fortune 500 company in the early days. They were very interested in Snowflake and asked when we would produce an on-premises version of the product. Benoit was in that meeting and politely responded: "You will go cloud before Snowflake goes on-premises."

Training: the MEDDPICC Process

As we grew, the MEDDPICC sales qualification process became the cornerstone of our sales qualification methodology. It was the process EMC trained me on. Snowflake board member John McMahon helped bring this framework to life in 1996, with Dick Dunkel and Jack Napoli, when he led sales at Parametric Technology Corporation (PTC) in Boston. MEDDPICC is an acronym made up of the eight principles of the sales qualification process. It was famous for its simplicity and depth. Essentially, they wanted to know why PTC won the deals it did, why it lost deals, and why deals would delay past their forecasted close date. They were looking for something that would be effective within large B2B customers with many stakeholders and approvals, who needed complex software solutions to solve their problems. MEDDPICC was a way of demystifying the sales qualification process and better predicting the potential of every sales opportunity. And when you plan to hire hundreds or thousands of sales people, you better have a process.

We incorporated the methodology at Snowflake, which included the following principles: using **M**etrics, understanding the **E**conomic buyer, understanding a customer's **D**ecision criteria, understanding their **D**ecision process, their **P**aper process (where so many deals fall through the cracks), **I**dentifying the customer's pain, identifying your **C**hampion within the customer's organization (every successful deal has one) and identifying your **C**ompetition—both within your customer's organization and outside. By knowing these steps, and incorporating the MEDDPICC methodology, sales reps have a better chance of accurately navigating the sales process and closing a deal. In detail, each principle should be applied in the following way:

- The **M**etrics should be clear. What are the customer's goals? Do they want to increase revenue, market share, efficiencies, and/or productivity? Do they understand the value your product provides? You want to discuss what you bring to the table in terms of solutions, so they can see how you will improve their metrics and help them make the case inside their organization for establishing a relationship with you.

- The **E**conomic buyer is the person with the authority to say "yes" or "no." They usually have their own budgets and can influence or determine the size of the deal. Not having them on board is a serious risk to landing a deal.

- The **D**ecision criteria has to do with the technical aspects of the solution you are selling. Does it provide enough value? Does your solution deliver what you say it does? Does it satisfy the customer's concerns around infrastructure, data security, and other features? Will it use up too much of the customer's resources to manage? Is your company a strong partner in the customer's industry? Every customer and their decision-makers will have their own criteria. Your sales reps must find out from the customer what criteria are important to them.

- Next, do you know the **D**ecision process within the customer? Who is involved? How do they evaluate and choose which company to work with? Is there a validation stage and an approval stage? When does that take place? What are their criteria?

- Is there a **P**aper process that you need to be aware of? A customer's procurement process can be a labyrinth of approval steps and one of the main reasons a deal can slip past its expected close date.

Look to **I**dentify the pain points inside the company. Is the pain great enough that they are motivated to evaluate competing solutions and choose one within a specific window of time? That's the kind of pain you are looking for in order to help them alleviate it. Without a pain point, there isn't the urgency to budget for and solve the problem.

Do you have a **C**hampion inside the company? Someone who is convinced your product is the best possible alternative and will promote it to their fellow stakeholders who will also see its value? Do your competitors have a champion? If so, who are they? How can your champion counter theirs?

And finally, who is your **C**ompetition? This includes competing vendors and the option of the customer developing their own solution to address their pain instead of choosing yours or that of your competitors'. I encourage our sales reps to focus on the benefits and strengths Snowflake offers and avoid denigrating the competition. Attacking a competitor's solution head on is just not an effective strategy.

But John goes further. When your sales reps eventually sell to an enterprise company, they need to think about who in the company they are talking to. He encouraged me to think of each stakeholder within the customer as having a sign on their forehead that says, "What's in it for me?" Once you know that, you need to speak their language and address their specific issues. If I'm selling to a software engineer, they will want to hear about features and functions. A VP of Engineering will want to know how your solution will make their people and processes more productive and help shorten their time to market. CXOs think in terms of increasing revenue, profitability, and market share, while reducing risk and costs. "If you can put it in those terms," John told me, "they'll listen. They're not gonna throw you out of their office."

The Trough of Disillusionment

Sales reps would get excited about joining Snowflake, and then six months in, some would start to ask themselves, "What did I get myself into?" If they were hired very early on, they were only selling the $500 evaluation agreements. If they were hired just after GA, their first six months focused on training, building a pipeline, and closing small deals. Sales reps are impatient, and that's usually a good thing. But it's a bad thing when they feel there's nothing they can do about it. You have to address this before and after hiring a sales rep. During recruitment, you have to stick to your plan of hiring people who demonstrate that they do well in the face of adversity. It's one thing to overcome obstacles but it's another to fight off an overall sense of disillusion.

Once they're hired, check in with them because the quickest exit happens after the shortest tenure. A sales rep is more likely to make a snap decision if they think they've made an honest mistake months after starting a new job. This couldn't be more true with younger professionals—the type of people we hired early on. The view that having a job for less than a few years was a negative on your resume ended decades ago. And having just one such experience is easy to explain to the next hiring manager, especially as a salesperson in a software startup. Young professionals know this, which can increase their level of risk-taking when starting a new job and increase their likelihood of leaving early, on a whim.

Your sales managers need to plan for this with their teams. They need to recognize that this is something brought on by the individual and short lived, so it's easy to address. A young sales rep needs insight and reassurance from their manager, who has more years in the industry and is closer to senior people in sales and other parts of your organization. They can pass on what they've heard about what strides are being made around the company while a disillusioned rep is waiting for their own rocket to lift off. This is also an opportunity to strengthen manager-rep relationships by building the trust that sales reps need to address any issue related to their job. Otherwise, a rep could make a snap decision and leave prematurely. If they stew over it long enough, they could end up confiding in a fellow rep instead of their manager. From there, more members of the team might consider leaving.

4

Target One Competitor, for Now

"Thank God for Redshift."

—Bob Muglia, CEO

AMAZON WEB SERVICES (AWS) launched its service in 2006. Organizations could rent virtual computers and storage in the cloud to store their data and run their software applications. When work began in 2012 to build Snowflake's cloud data warehouse, it was obvious to our founders that Snowflake should run on top of AWS as our first cloud infrastructure partner.

The engineers were working hard to develop our product when the announcement came. AWS launched Redshift—their own data warehouse for the cloud. We were still three years from GA. Worse, AWS charged rock-bottom prices for Redshift. It was practically included with the price they charged for their computing-as-a-service, which was the real cost we would have to pass on to our customers for eventually running Snowflake on AWS. This was not a new tactic in the tech industry. Long before the cloud was commercially available, behemoth hardware companies such as IBM created their own databases and structured their pricing to make it look like their software was free to customers. Not long after, in the 1990s, there was a series of application software companies that became the dominant players in their tech sectors. Many of them had solutions that didn't work well but they had incredible influence over customers and deep pockets to market in ways that obscured their product deficiencies. Either way, these tech vendors had established a history of getting customers to adopt substandard technology in order to close a deal.

AWS was already the dominant player in cloud computing and storage. Soon after, they took aim at the software stack, offering a data warehouse and additional products. With Redshift commercially available, everyone—including the investor community—thought AWS was going to eat our lunch. "Why would we invest in Snowflake only to have AWS kick the crap out of you?" That was their attitude. Yet, the reality of AWS crushing Snowflake before our product was still in development jarred us. Benoit considered heavily the option of packing up and going home. He wouldn't have been the first tech visionary to realize that even the best product from a startup couldn't survive whatever came from a behemoth of a competitor.

But then two things emerged that transformed Redshift from being our biggest competitor to the product that helped jumpstart Snowflake's commercial success. AWS signed more than 1,000 Redshift customers in just nine months. Interestingly, AWS did not acquire these customers from the existing on-premises data warehouse market. They were organizations choosing the cloud, which offered theoretically unlimited amounts of computing and storage. There were smaller organizations that didn't already have acres of their own on-premises hardware configurations. They didn't have an aircraft carrier to turn around. AWS revealed there was a market for cloud data warehousing. It also made a serious mistake. In its rush to offer a cloud data warehouse, it adapted ParAccel, a database designed for on-premises computing environments, called it Redshift, and offered it in the cloud.

When the business world started to realize that the cloud could be as safe or even more safe than their own data centers, software companies made haste to produce cloud versions of their existing solutions. Many of them also rushed that process, understandably so. Simply porting an on-premises solution had its benefits. Customers could shutter their own data centers and simply access those same solutions via the Internet. But the benefits of a ported solution didn't extend much beyond that. Those solutions failed to take advantage of the enormous resources cloud computing offered. A solution built for the cloud, such as Snowflake, could do that.

Fortunately, Snowflake's engineers continued to develop our data warehouse for the next two to three years. Redshift's appeal grew immensely. In addition to seeding customers that were cloud-first, AWS started to disrupt the traditional data warehouse market. It was much less expensive than a legacy data warehouse, so customers used Redshift alongside those legacy solutions. It's rare that a large customer will execute a wholesale dump of an incumbent product. Instead, they will buy a competing product for a few specific features. It's costly and cumbersome but it can start a much-needed look at a staged migration of all its computing solutions to the cloud.

Enter Bob Muglia

Bob arrived in June 2014. His biggest career accomplishment before Snowflake was more than two decades at Microsoft. For his last six years there, he was the company's president of server and tools business. During his tenure, that division nearly doubled revenue to $17 billion and nearly doubled operating income to more than $6 billion.

As a career technologist, Bob recognized the brilliance of building a data warehouse specifically for the cloud. He also understood how unique Snowflake's architecture was and how it differed from other data warehouses and databases that were built for on-premises environments. He was a huge boost to Snowflake's evolving legitimacy and it showed. He often delivered the keynote at many of our live events designed to create demand for the product. He has a penetrating mind and unending enthusiasm. He would captivate hundreds of prospects every time he took the stage. People got what he was saying and how he said it. His enthusiasm peaked when his presentations reached the point at which he would detail the nuts and bolts of Snowflake. He would nearly pop out of his shoes at his first utterance of the word "architecture." He brought that same level of excitement when talking to customers and participating in other marketing programs that the marketing team developed once Denise came onboard later as chief marketing officer.

A lot of CEOs want everyone to think they know a lot about every function of a business. Most don't. Bob is a super intelligent guy, but he freely admitted he didn't know much about running sales organizations. He was honest about that, so he deferred to John McMahon and me. John talked to me about how to work with Bob, as the head of sales. He told me what issues to bring to Bob, how to give him my honest opinion on things, and avoid feeling like I was second fiddle to the CEO. You want to basically have a relationship with the CEO, John explained, where he's the CEO, but I express my full opinion as far as what I see going on in the company. Whatever decision Bob makes, that's fine. He's the CEO. But a head of sales shouldn't shortchange themselves or their opinions by failing to tell their CEO what they see going on. John's point was that a lot of first-time CROs don't see themselves at the same level as the CEO. So, they don't give them all the honest feedback they should. And that's really not what a good CEO wants. They want to know everything that's going on.

Snowflake vs. Redshift

It was June 2015 when Snowflake's cloud-built data warehouse became commercially available. It still lacked many staple features that customers raised with us during the product's development. But that didn't stop the sales team from pounding the phones and the pavement. AWS Redshift was still winning tons of accounts. We were competing against their sales reps and losing most of the time. These accounts had deployed Redshift only recently and the product was working for them. Also, even if a customer thought Redshift and Snowflake were a tie, or Snowflake had an edge over Redshift, they would not choose us. We had fewer than 100 employees. AWS had been in business for more than 10 years, had thousands working for them, and was the anointed tech child of Amazon. Customers often choose stability over a startup.

Bob was on the East Coast, attending sales calls with Vince Trotta, who turned to Bob and said: "You know, I think these Redshift accounts are the best thing that ever happened to us. All of these accounts are gonna come around 18 months from now, when they run out of gas on Redshift and we're going to win them over." That's exactly what started to happen. Redshift customers demanded more of the product, which was still limited by its legacy architecture designed for on-premises environments. "They did a classic (Jeff) Bezos deal," Bob once said. "Amazon didn't buy the company. They bought the codebase. And they took the database, called it Redshift, stuffed it in the cloud, and priced it dirt cheap. It reinvigorated the data warehouse market because the product actually worked until you hit the wall, and then it was a terrible product."

Redshift couldn't scale to handle ever-increasing workloads that required more data and more computing. The AWS computing power was there but its own data warehouse couldn't exploit that resource beyond what it was designed to do inside customers' own data centers. We started to win those accounts because Redshift couldn't scale. It was the perfect competitor for us. A behemoth and well-respected technology provider that was first to market with great technology for on-demand storage and computing in the cloud. Then it offered a data warehouse on top of that foundation but one that would eventually run out of gas. Later on, at a Snowflake sales kickoff event that included about 30 of us, Bob stepped onto the two-foot-high stage, sat down on its edge, held the cordless mic and uttered in a tone lower than normal from him, "Thank God for Redshift."

Choose One or Two Adversaries and Win Over Their Business

Snowflake separated compute from storage, creating access to the near-unlimited data storage and computing resources the AWS infrastructure platform provided. Snowflake could also ingest JSON data natively. These two attributes alone helped us get our first 100 customers. These customers had few staff, and their products generated a ton of data.

Many companies also began to buy Redshift and use it in conjunction with Hadoop. They would store their raw data in Hadoop, which included semi-structured data such as JSON, and then extract it into a Redshift data warehouse in order to analyze it. This required a lot of time and money to operate two solutions in order to store and analyze data. Snowflake could replace both of those products as a single solution. That also meant those customers had already started down the path of adopting cloud computing, which was our number one criterion for selling Snowflake in early GA. That was our use case, and we started replacing these products at existing Redshift customers and winning against Redshift in new accounts.

Like we did at Snowflake, focus on a competitor that has the right vision but a technology yours could surpass. It also has to be a product that's easy for you to replace. Both Redshift and Snowflake run on AWS. It was the most straightforward migration we faced. All a customer had to do was direct its data stored in AWS away from Redshift and toward Snowflake. Migrating data from Hadoop to Snowflake took more time and effort but it was much easier than migrating off of large and entrenched legacy products such as Teradata, Vertica, and Netezza. Those projects could take a year, or longer, before Snowflake was up and running. All big migrations can take a while because no two projects are alike, requiring a fair amount of consulting work to complete the migration.

Like all software, your product was designed to address a number of deficiencies of at least one competing solution. As your product is undergoing development, choose one or two competitors that meet most or all of the following criteria:

1. Market leader
2. Lacks many features customers need
3. Requires a large upfront investment
4. Needs a number of people to manage
5. Requires complementary products to address new business needs
6. Was adapted from older technology
7. Is priced low or free when purchased with other products
8. Is easily replaced by your product

Of all eight, your targeted competitor(s) should have a significant share of your total addressable market (TAM). Otherwise, you will risk positioning your product to compete with market laggards and confine your product to competing for a small portion of the market owned by those laggards. Your product will lack many features initially, but you can overshadow that shortfall by providing features and functionality that your competitors don't offer and that your customers value more than the features your competitors do provide. When it comes to investment, making it easy for a potential customer to trial your product for little money will help you seed the market fast. Charge a nominal fee for a trial of your product so prospects have a commitment to peeking under the hood. But make it easy for them to get rolling with a trial that could start a migration to your product or at least deploy your product alongside their existing deployment of your competitors' product. If the competing products you're targeting are free, don't worry. That shows customers that the vendors of those products don't value the product, so why should they? And if you can easily swap their product for yours, a customer will at least give you the opportunity to pitch to them. Once we developed partnerships with systems integrators and developed our professional services organization, Snowflake's marketing team developed a program targeting Teradata—one of the prominent legacy data warehouse providers. Teradata and other such products required huge investment, large support teams, and eventually needed Hadoop and/or Redshift alongside to handle storing and analyzing more of its customers' data. Simply getting Snowflake deployed in these accounts to handle some of a customer's data led to large migrations we could support.

Going After Larger Deals: A Turning Point

As a startup, there is always a danger that you will disappoint a customer or that your technology might not be ready to handle the volume and complexity that comes with working with large enterprises. We focused on making our customers incredibly successful and then making them advisors to our product road map via our customer advisory boards, so that they too had a stake in Snowflake's future. Those first few large customers were also our partners. Once your product is GA, the level of input you need from your customers to develop new product features doesn't end, or even dissipate. Ensure their continued feedback. Make them referenceable to future prospects. And minimize churn, so those customers love the relationship as much as they do your product.

Most successful startups move up from calling on small-to-medium-sized businesses and then on to bigger companies and eventually break into the enterprise space. It wasn't long until prospects of many types became interested in Snowflake. We were about a year into GA and we were in sales motions with organizations that weren't just ad tech and online gaming companies. Others had on-premises data warehouses that were at least a decade old and inquired of us about adding significant functionality to our product. We took a balanced approach to these opportunities. We wanted the business because we knew these types of deals would eventually come our way. But we had a small amount of resources to help customers get up and running on Snowflake. If it wasn't a transition from Redshift to Snowflake, the challenges included developing a method to port a legacy data warehouse to Snowflake, moving petabytes of data into Snowflake and integrating a customer's many complementary solutions with Snowflake, to name a few. At this point in time, we were still using our pre-sales engineers to help new customers, who were already in the cloud, to get up and running with Snowflake. Safe to say, we chose this next group of customers carefully. We didn't have a professional services organization yet, we couldn't overrun our engineers managing too many migration projects, and we didn't have any partners that had experience yet migrating a legacy data warehouse to Snowflake.

The first group of customers produced wins and losses. If we won or lost a deal, it was no mystery as to why. We sold our product to an online gaming company that used Redshift for storage and analytics. But Redshift couldn't handle JSON data and the customer needed that capability. They added Snowflake to their data strategy, making them our first $100,000 customer. Migrating from Redshift was fairly straightforward. Similarly, an online cybersecurity and fraud prevention company became a Snowflake customer. They too had a ton of JSON files and needed a product that could transform that data into a program that their instance of Redshift could handle, so they bought Snowflake. These weren't the most provocative deals. But these early customer opportunities proved Snowflake could add value even to customers that continued to run Redshift but placed a lot of value on the unique benefits that Snowflake brought to data warehouse technology.

A customer that produces home, beauty, and healthcare products was another story entirely. It took their current system two days to compute a certain query on their data. It took less than two minutes with Snowflake to perform that same query. How could we lose such an opportunity? We did. We couldn't plug into any of their other systems. A data warehouse requires a number of complementary data products to get data in and analyze that data for business insights. We had yet to develop one connector to even the most popular ETL (extract, transform, and load) and BI (business intelligence) tools. That was our next engineering talk—building connectors. But our time spent with that company was not wasted. We proved we could provide enormous performance value even though we had yet to integrate with their systems that they used for data analytics. They understood, as a startup, we needed time to develop integrations. And we understood "no" from a prospect is only "no" at that moment. A prospect stops being a prospect only when they become a customer. We made an impression, so our time spent on that missed opportunity created value for Snowflake.

A global software corporation was the first significant customer that expressed interest in our product. The software giant decided to move off of its Netezza solution and started using Redshift. That signified they had already chosen to develop a cloud strategy, and their data warehousing was going in that direction. Shortly thereafter, they started trialing Snowflake. I ended up selling to them because they had a desperate problem that was a perfect fit for us to solve without overrunning our company in the process. At first, they didn't believe our product could do what we said it would. They were one of AWS's first Redshift customers and generated hundreds of terabytes of data each week. But they could only load new data over the weekend, which soon became three- and four-day weekends. We came along and spun up 2,000 servers for four hours on Fridays to load all that data at once. The database administrator who had to babysit the weekend data loads prior to Snowflake arriving on the scene was an overweight chain-smoker. Thanks to Snowflake he quit cigarettes and lost a bunch of weight. The company became our first major customer because what we did offer was not just impressive, similar to what other customers experienced, but it was crucial that this company implement our technology immediately. Even though the customer was still using both Snowflake and Redshift, they had already started down the path of migrating off a legacy data warehouse. By implementing Redshift, they began their move to the cloud. Redshift already paved the way for Snowflake with pure cloud customers. Now, it was paving the way for us with on-premises customers willing to commit to the cloud—the next phase of our sales strategy.

A Boston-based company became another large customer. It was a mobile marketing and analytics company and was attempting a 500-terabyte Vertica migration. Snowflake would turn out to be their foray into cloud data warehousing. That customer would also turn out to be one of the more pivotal customers in our history. The company had a fundamental problem and they were desperate to find an alternative data warehouse. It was probably one of the most expensive database migrations Snowflake ever did. They needed us to do something called reclustering and we didn't have that capability yet. It was a hard thing to implement, but we had a customer that was willing to pay us to develop that feature. Our founders and the engineering team were convinced that it would benefit a lot of big customers going forward. It took 18 months. When we finished, data deletions could take place at the same time new data was being added to the same data table. We had to make major architectural changes to Snowflake to implement reclustering. "Theirs was the problem that helped us mature the system and capabilities that made Snowflake a world class database," Bob said. That project was incredibly significant but just the right size for Snowflake to handle at the time. John McMahon said that project pushed our engineers hard but allowed Snowflake to later land a huge financial services customer. This legacy migration could have been at our entire expense, but the customer saw immense value in financing a major upgrade to Snowflake's architecture and functionality, and we knew what that meant for us with future customers.

As a startup, don't relegate your opportunities to the limits imposed on you at any one time. There are many ways to advance your product and your company once you reveal and quantify the potential value gained, and who will benefit the most by committing the resources to achieving that milestone. As we've said previously, just time these projects right so they don't run your engineering team into the ground or take your product in the wrong direction.

Consumption-Based Pricing

Snowflake was not like other SaaS products when it first became GA. Those solutions had subscription-based pricing. You pay a fee, typically per month, based on what modules or functionality of the software your organization uses, how many users access the system, and how much data you store. From day one, Snowflake offered usage- or consumption-based pricing. You only pay for the data storage and computing resources you use. We were one of the first SaaS companies to standardize on consumption-based pricing. But our data warehouse had features that made that type of pricing even more attractive. Snowflake was built to allow users to instantly spin up as much computing power as needed and turn off that horsepower just as quickly once a query returned the results of analyzing a ton of data. This is the same for other data workloads that Snowflake is capable of delivering. Public utilities pioneered usage-based pricing. In recent decades, this pricing strategy has taken hold of other industries, such as insurance, and has given rise to new services such as ride hailing and single-ride mobility rentals.

This pricing strategy was a critical component of securing large deals with enterprises that deployed traditional data warehouse technology in the cloud or inside their own on-premises data warehouses. Many SaaS companies now offer consumption-based pricing. But it's a strategy that can also be tricky. Customers don't know in advance exactly how much computing power they will need over one, two, or three years with a SaaS product such as Snowflake. Since going GA, our engineers have added a number of features so customers can predict, allocate, monitor, and control Snowflake usage across their different departments. This helps customers fit consumption pricing into traditional forecasting and budgeting practices that still govern an organization's financial practices.

In addition to the customer benefits associated with consumption pricing, there are at least three significant impacts to the business processes of SaaS companies that offer such pricing. The first is how you must structure your sales forecasts. Snowflake does not realize product revenue once a sales contract is signed. It only hits our books when customers use our product. Whether we sign them up for a $500 trial or $100 million, multi-year contract with discounted pricing, we realize zero revenue until they start using Snowflake. This requires other tools and processes to accurately predict and report revenue as a private or public company. We were one of the first to offer consumption pricing, and that made us one of the first to deploy data science teams in our sales and finance organizations to help accurately forecast revenue.

Secondly, and related to this, we compensate our sales reps partly when a customer signs a contract but mostly at a rate that aligns with when the customer consumes storage and computing resources. This is critical for a couple of reasons. It aligns our sales revenue with sales compensation. Every CFO can agree this makes good business sense. More importantly, we have complete responsibility for our customer's success. Prior to SaaS, enterprise software was solely designed to be shipped on disc, tape, or other physical formats and installed in a customer's own data center. There was zero accountability from the vendor to ensure that the customer achieved the first hurdle—a successful installation. Sounds easy but it wasn't, and a lot of expensive software purchases literally remained on a shelf never to be installed. Then the software had to become operational. This could take months or even years. Finally, it had to connect to the customer's other solutions. Put all of this together and it required customers to spend huge dollars on services with the software vendor or with a third-party tech services firm. The standard in the industry was a three-to-one spend ratio. For every dollar spent on software, you had to spend three dollars on consulting to get it up and running. SaaS computing alleviated much of this but introduced its own financial issues. SaaS vendors still offer subscription pricing. These are monthly fees charged whether you use the product or not, and whether you max out your pre-purchased usage every month or not. In both scenarios, the vendor and their sales reps have almost zero accountability once the contract is signed. The customer has paid for the software or the customer is bound to paying its monthly SaaS subscription. From there, the sales rep will understandably move on to the next opportunity.

Finally, with consumption pricing, the vendor and its sales organization are bound to their customers for as long as they are customers. At Snowflake, our reps help customers get up and running with our product, show them how to efficiently exploit the technology, and help reveal additional use cases that would benefit from using the product. In many cases, organizations have revealed new market opportunities and created new lines of business thanks to Snowflake. This business model transforms the sales relationship. It leads to higher customer satisfaction, reduced churn, and more customer input and influence over our product road map.

5

Scaling with Partners

"You need friends."

—Chris Degnan

BUSINESS ECOSYSTEMS—IT'S WHERE our scale comes from. No matter how fast we scaled our sales organization, our partners helped deliver more business than we could ever do on our own. They're out there talking about us every day, trying to make money with their own services and solutions that are complementary to Snowflake. Some of them provide products that integrate with Snowflake. Other partners use Snowflake as a platform to build software on top of our technology. Others, such as service providers, help customers implement Snowflake, migrate a customer's legacy solutions to Snowflake, and build products for customers that integrate with our technology. That's the mark of a platform, and Snowflake was fast becoming one. We can't provide all of these services and solutions. Snowflake relies on its partners, and they rely on us.

Be Quick and Act Big

We jump-started our alliances in 2015 and just prior to GA. We hired people who understood the technical aspects of product integrations that we desperately needed between Snowflake and other as-a-service vendors. Our alliances team was skilled at finding key complementary technology providers, revealing to them the value of such a partnership and detailing a successful go-to-market strategy with us. We would walk into meetings as if Snowflake was a billion-dollar company. "You need us," we told our partners. We weren't faking it. We couldn't walk in with low confidence because we were small. We didn't care about the size of our company because we were confident we had the people and technology that would deliver value to our partners. We continued to punch above our weight, creating partnerships with companies of all sizes. Many of them had no interest in us at first. As a startup, they thought we would likely fade away, but we convinced them otherwise. Without our partners, we would never have received the attention we did in the market early on. This brought us credibility, and we provided our joint customers additional value. No technology company rose to great heights without a solid business ecosystem.

Create your Virtual Salesforce Through Partnerships

As we mentioned previously, our customers desperately needed Snowflake to integrate with the emerging and popular business intelligence (BI) tools. Every major data warehouse had a BI tool connected to it. We didn't, because we had customers early on that didn't require such a tool. These solutions convert the analytics from Snowflake into easily understood graphical analysis. In essence, Snowflake is the engine and a BI tool is the dashboard. These dashboards reveal to executives how the company is performing across any area of the business. They can offer descriptive, predictive, and prescriptive insights on where to take the company next.

The first cloud BI company to build a Snowflake connector was **Looker.** This was about a year before we created our alliances team. We shared a venture capital investor, who introduced us to one of Looker's cofounders. We started getting both our sales teams together, co-marketing together, and integrating our two products. Looker and Snowflake were both founded in 2012, so we had the same upside by partnering with one another. Looker was faster to market with their product, which made sense. Building a cloud data warehouse from scratch was an intense and complicated endeavor. Once the two products had a connection, we would bring Looker to a lot of our customers and they would do the same. As the partnership progressed, we created a product development road map to ensure Looker and Snowflake together was the ideal solution for customers. Our joint customers also used Looker's suite of application programming interfaces (APIs) to build their own custom data applications. A telecommunications company built an ad revenue monetization portal for all of its advertisers, which sat on top of Looker and Snowflake.

During our five-year relationship, our co-marketing and co-selling strategies resulted in a third of our customers also using Looker. As new reps came on board at Looker or Snowflake, they met their rep counterparts. On the marketing side, we sponsored each other's events. If I wanted to talk about Looker's go-to-market strategy, I'd give the cofounder a call. When Looker entered Japan first, they shared that strategy with us. They also showed us how they built their partner program. "We were two independents in this category, and we wanted to grow like crazy, so let's help each other," they said. They introduced us to other ecosystem partners that offered non-competing technologies to Looker that would also add value to Snowflake's technology ecosystem. A lot of good things came from that relationship. When Google finalized its acquisition of Looker in 2020, that basically ended our relationship. Google's BigQuery product was in direct competition with our solution, and Google only saw it that way.

Next came our partnership with **Tableau**—a much bigger and direct competitor to Looker. "Go make friends with Tableau," we told the alliances team, and they did. You'd think that would be problematic for both partners, but it wasn't. Partners would be more wary of your partnership if you didn't align with their competitors. In such an environment, everyone benefits, including the customer. When we're all competing for their business, they will ask who we recommend for a BI tool. We respond by saying who we partner with and let them make their decision based on their review of those products.

In addition to our BI partnerships, there was another huge hole we had to fill on the other side of our technology for customers. Before running queries on the data in Snowflake, and before visualizing that data with a BI tool, customers had to get their data into Snowflake. That required an extract, transfer, and load (ETL) solution. We struck partnerships with Informatica, a market veteran, and Fivetran, a new entrant to the ETL business. These partners, and others like them, were crucial to establishing Snowflake as part of an end-to-end solution. Sure, we positioned our solution as being at the center of an organization's data strategy. But no solution on its own will pique interest unless you can show your go-to-market strategy is absolutely customer focused. Without these partners, solving problems on either side of Snowflake would be similar to buying a car without a gas tank and a dashboard. In the end, you can't get to a billion dollars in revenue on your own.

Coopetition with the 8,000 lb Rhinos

Ken Chestnut built the partner business at AWS and helped establish our relationship with them soon after we were GA. But Redshift was always hovering in the background, complicating that relationship. Andy Jassy was the CEO of AWS at that time and viewed Redshift as his baby. He knew we were targeting Redshift customers who were having problems with that product. Each year, Ken would tell us that AWS was going to announce new technology for Redshift at its annual re:Invent conference. He called it the "Snowflake killer." Each year, they didn't kill us. But there were times we inadvertently or deliberately gave them a reason to.

In 2016, AWS was still the only cloud infrastructure provider that Snowflake operated on. Our board of directors decided then that we should no longer charge our customers a commission on AWS data storage. To accomplish this, we would simply pass through the price AWS charged us. In that press release, we also took aim at all of our top competitors, stating that Snowflake now offered the most inexpensive storage for a data warehouse. Redshift was one of them. Bob took the high road and let AWS know a day before the announcement what was coming. It didn't make much of a difference. Days later, at our weekly all-hands meeting, Bob said with a half smile: "We poked the bear, and the bear didn't like that." It strained the relationship, but the relationship survived. Trying to partner with a technology partner that is a thousand times larger than you, and has a product that competes with yours, does not mean you can't be partners. You just have to find that one thing that provides value to both companies, which will survive if you always compete in good faith. If you don't compete in good faith, you'll get what you deserve.

Despite this, AWS became one of our closest partners. Ken always said AWS is customer obsessed and it will do whatever is in the customer's best interest. Snowflake followed that same mantra. AWS reps selling Redshift despised us for a while. But their reps who sold AWS infrastructure, computing and storage, thought differently. When Snowflake won against Redshift, AWS also won because Snowflake ran on AWS infrastructure. "Think of AWS as one hundred different companies, with each product team basically running their own profit and loss," Ken said. Our product complemented other AWS products such as SageMaker—one of AWS's machine learning solutions. Our ability to help make AWS sell non-competing products alongside Snowflake, and someone like Ken as our champion inside AWS, allowed the relationship to survive then and strengthen over the years.

What really solidified the partnership early on was a sales opportunity in which our presence helped AWS beat out their biggest competitors. Ken and I would brainstorm around how to go after enterprise customers that were beginning to move large data workloads out of their legacy on-premises data centers and into the cloud. Sure, Redshift was a data warehouse option for the customer. But if they favored Snowflake over Redshift, and favored other data warehouses available from AWS's cloud infrastructure competitors Microsoft Azure and Google Cloud Platform, we could help them win the infrastructure business. "I could always go to AWS leadership and demonstrate that Snowflake is not always competing against us," Ken said. "They're driving net-new business to us."

From my perspective, Ken once made a move that could have gotten him fired. AWS gives its partners credits toward their computing and storage usage to offset the cost of a partner conducting a proof of concept (POC) to a potential AWS customer. Depending on the size of the deal, a POC can cost hundreds of thousands of dollars and gives a customer a fairly solid understanding, before they purchase, as to how a software vendor's product will alleviate issues with their existing solution and what impact it will have on their business. AWS and Snowflake had an enterprise customer evaluating Redshift, Snowflake, and BigQuery—Google's version of a cloud data warehouse. An independent consulting partner helped conduct the initial evaluation of all three products. Snowflake came in first, followed by BigQuery. Redshift came in third. Next was the POC. But AWS had a policy not to fund Snowflake's POCs because we pitched against Redshift. But in this deal, that meant Google would possibly fund the Snowflake POC if it meant the customer chose Snowflake as the data warehouse and Google for computing and storage. Herein lies the issue. If a cloud infrastructure provider already knows that their data warehouse has ranked below that of a SaaS vendor's solution, they risk losing a vastly larger part of the deal—the computing and storage. Ken approved funding for the Snowflake POC and the customer chose Snowflake and AWS. "It was worth tens of millions of dollars, if not hundreds of millions of dollars in revenue (to AWS)," Ken recalled.

His decision to help us definitely moved the needle in our partnership. And honestly, Amazon has made a lot of smart decisions in our partnership since those early days. The key to our joint success was the hotline between Ken and Snowflake. As soon as one of us got wind of an issue, our first move was to de-escalate whatever angst had emerged between AWS and Snowflake people outside of our little domain. "Chris, Denise, and their alliances team understood the importance of our partnership," Ken said. "We trusted one another and having those unofficial channels meant we could figure out those tricky situations and how to navigate them." There was too much at stake. If a large enterprise is migrating 10 or 20 percent of its data to the cloud, that's a big opportunity for both of us. Knowing one day that it could be 100 percent kept us absolutely customer-focused.

* * * *

In 2018, we launched Snowflake on Microsoft Azure. It was early days for Microsoft's cloud offering intended to rival AWS. As a former executive there, Bob Muglia had access to the people who mattered. No one at Snowflake knew anything about Microsoft Azure, so Bob opened an office in Washington near its headquarters and staffed it with former Microsoft people to run Snowflake on Azure. As it should have, this all came about due to customer demand. We had a massive opportunity with a company in the retail industry. Understandably, they would not allow any of their technology or data to live within a cloud infrastructure provider that was a subsidiary of Amazon. We were now partners with Microsoft, and that relationship created tensions with AWS, but not for long. It actually strengthened our relationship with them. We were growing and diversifying.

Microsoft also realized we were expanding fast. I told them that our continued growth had a lot to do with our AWS partnership. Satya Nadella, CEO of Microsoft, got involved, and we ended up signing a large agreement with them. We taught them a lot about cloud stability and scalability issues. We were very much co-selling with Microsoft and brought them a lot of business. Later, we launched Snowflake on Google Cloud Platform for the same reason—customer demand. Google sees us as a competitor, so we don't have the same relationship with them. AWS is still the market leader for cloud infrastructure, with Azure in second and Google a distant third. The success we have with each of those partners aligns with their own success. That correlation, I think, has to do more with how each of them views their partnerships.

Why a Large and Respectful Ecosystem Matters

Having many partners matters. The only way to grow from $1 million in revenue to $10 million, and then to $100 million, $1 billion, and eventually $10 billion is to have a genuine computing platform with an enormous partner ecosystem. The biggest companies in the world are truly partner-focused. The Microsoft Partner Network is one of the largest business ecosystems on the planet. Companies around the world have made a lot of money implementing Microsoft. Snowflake's network includes technology providers, resellers, and also global systems integrators, which help customers implement your platform. Most importantly, you have to develop relationships with other technology providers and make it easy for them to develop their software and applications on top of your platform. That's a sign that you've reached the next level with your ecosystem and a topic we will discuss in a later chapter. You need friends, you need partners, and you need complementary products and services that other companies can provide. We at Snowflake understood this and started building our ecosystem early on. "When you're an early-stage startup, find a big brother or big sister to partner with. In those early days, Snowflake did a great job of leveraging AWS and our position in the market," Ken recalled.

6

Scale Your Culture

"Put customers first."

—Snowflake's number 1 value

OUR FIRST EFFORTS to develop our sense of culture were what a small team of engineers and sales folks desperately needed. Back then, we focused on the interpersonal. We worked so hard at coding and prospecting that we needed other things at Snowflake to look forward to. We represented a number of different countries, and each wore a few hats, but everyone would show up to the events we organized. Our culture was built upon camaraderie, mainly. Soon after Bob arrived in 2014, we decided to codify the Snowflake values. At our weekly all-hands meetings, Bob would ask what was really important to us. The engineers had a big say in what our values should be. They were here from the very beginning, but everyone participated. It was the right time.

Soon after we went GA, we began hiring sales reps who worked remotely across the United States. We opened up small offices in major metropolitan areas where sales teams started to grow in numbers. We were expanding at our Silicon Valley headquarters as well. We had moved out of our small offices in downtown San Mateo and occupied two floors of a larger building just a block away. We kept that office space as we started to further expand into a nine-floor building right across the street. We took over the ground floor, then the fifth, and eventually the ninth.

We were the youngest people, by a few decades, that traversed the lobby. Often, we opted to take the stairs instead of waiting more than five minutes for one of the two elevators to arrive. The immediate surroundings of that downtown has always had a high concentration of elderly people, and we were in the midst of taking over a building full of doctors' offices.

As we grew, our efforts couldn't reach every Snowflake. Even the annual company-wide ski trip was in jeopardy because it became too costly and lasted three days—an eternity for sales reps. In addition, the culture we had did not address anything beyond the mutual respect we developed for each other. We needed a code, something we could hold ourselves and each other accountable to—one that would also serve our mission.

Creating Your Values

The earlier you establish your company's values, the better. When is it too soon? If it's just engineers at your company, it's too soon. You're still focused on one goal, developing a product, which is a crucial element to influencing your values. Software engineers come from all over the world to work in Silicon Valley. They represent a diverse mix of cultures, which is integral to this process. But engineers, no matter their cultural background, represent just one of many groups in a startup—emotionally, spiritually, ethically, and intellectually. In the meantime, you should still develop a culture of camaraderie similar to what we did for Snowflake. By the time we embarked on developing our values, we had a few admin staff, a finance person, and of course, sales reps, who couldn't be any more different than software engineers. When is it too late? If your company is more than about 50–75 people, or you're already experiencing geographic sprawl, the process to make every voice heard could delay codifying your values.

How many values should you have? As many that will define your culture and define how you treat your customers, your jobs, and each other. At the same time, you don't want to create such a list that your employees can't remember the title for each one. Otherwise, your values will resemble the length and style of a legal statute. How long should each one be? The title of each value should be between two and four words, with no less than three supporting sentences and no more than five. Three represents many things in every culture. For this exercise, a beginning, middle, and end. Five is about the most a person can take in and still walk away with the essence of each value. Keep each value description under 50 words but try to keep them all of similar length so as not to emphasize one over another. How you order them could take care of that.

Snowflake's Values

Over the course of 18 months, and after a lot of discussion (maybe too much), we settled on eight values for Snowflake. Three of them preserve the unspoken culture we had in those early years. The other five serve our mission, encapsulating how we strategize and execute as individuals and as an enterprise. Listed below are the titles of each one. Short description of each value can be found on our website. How we at Snowflake live each value is detailed below. Except for the first value, they are in no specific order.

Put customers first. Our sales team lives by this value but so does the rest of our company. You don't have to be in a customer-facing role in order to constantly serve them. For example, engineers must consistently deliver new product features and functionality that help customers reveal new insights about their business, best serve their customers, and save them money. We are always adding features that will increase performance and streamline how much computing and storage resources our customers need to get more done—especially if it means they will spend less with us. Marketers must know the product and how to position it so prospects can quickly and easily see the value from what's on our website, in our ebooks, and what's being communicated at our live events. What we say is a promise, and we have to make good on that. Our finance and accounting team is a big part of this, as well. We offer a consumption-based product because our customers should only pay for what they use. We also want our customers to plan what they spend and spend what they planned. Our legal team is tasked with many responsibilities, including making the purchase process as streamlined as possible. Everything our professional services team does rolls up to one goal: make customers successful. They and our sales team are who customers rely on the most—before, during, and after they become customers. In essence, they are more partners than customers, and each relationship requires our very best. For all of us on every team, the needs of the customer drive our behavior from the inception of a Snowflake strategy to its execution and delivery.

Integrity always. With customers, partners, and among ourselves, this is about honesty and respect in everything we do. If everyone is nodding in a meeting but you're not clear, or you disagree, be upfront but sincere. Input is the most powerful when it's direct, polite, and gets others to pause and give thought. Otherwise, if what's proposed goes unchallenged, then a failed sales opportunity or a marketing program, for example, will be no surprise. If you're uncomfortable, speak up anyway. This is especially important in a startup where nearly everyone has equity in the form of pre-IPO stock options. Such a financial benefit can also be a reason for many to stay quiet. An integrity-infused workplace also means there should be no chance of reprisal for anyone being open and thoughtful. On the flip side, remain informed, which is another way to respect other professionals. An evidence-based question will not only elicit a great response but will convey value to others in the form of new information. At the same time, stay clear of name-dropping to win a debate. The early days of a startup create professional relationships between employees who ascend to the highest levels of the company in later years. There are also those who are most effective as first-line managers or individual contributors with significant responsibilities. Both groups retain significant influence because they had access to executive management when your company was small. Avoid these baseless claims: "Well, I bet this senior vice president would agree with me" or "What would our CFO say about this?" These devious tactics are more damaging than keeping quiet when someone has a legitimate concern that needs to be discussed. When consensus does result in a decision, everyone involved should exhibit the integrity to support it, commit fully to execute on it, and yet provide any valid concerns as the strategy evolves and approaches its execution.

Think big. Be a driver, not a passenger. Why not? In a startup, nearly anything is possible. When those who need to be involved decide on something, we don't look for additional input or shelve it until next quarter. We start executing at that moment. We go as big as we can and spend what we can afford (or just over). For startups, this is a must. We managed Snowflake's partner program as if we were the biggest kid on the block. Our founders and engineers didn't build our product from the ground up to win some back-alley neighborhood drag race. They were out to win Formula 1 by a country mile. As our competition continues to catch up on our product innovations from years ago, our engineering team continues to innovate, keeping the competition in our rearview mirror. Instead of adopting the startup norm of the triple, triple, double, double for annual sales revenue for our first four years, Mike Speiser enshrined a triple, triple, triple, double, double strategy. We delivered on that and then some. Denise and her team continue to deliver compelling company and product messaging and content, live programs on a global scale, and customer stories that drive qualified sales leads with response rates that dramatically and consistently outpace industry standards. What we have written for this value on our website sums it all up: Plan to win, play to win, and expect to win.

Be excellent. This must happen in order to deliver on Think big. Too often, professionals kick off a project with all the vigor and excitement it deserves. As it progresses, their commitment can wane. A startup that operates with high intensity and urgency isn't for everyone. People have bursts of energy and moments of burnout. What happens next? The 80–20 curse kicks in. Instead of delivering something 100 percent of what it can be, we get to 80 percent quality and deliver only on that. People and teams that allow this to happen have terms to justify their inactions: "It's good enough." "It's great enough." "It's perfectly good." Years after we went GA, our second CEO Frank Slootman arrived. He held monthly all-hands meetings for the entire company. At one of those first meetings, he said, "We don't do 'okay' at Snowflake." He couldn't have made his point any clearer, and he created a level of pride and quality in everything we do. We're only human, and we can get tired and frustrated with a project, ushering in the dreaded 80–20 curse. But lazy work can destroy a company from the inside out. Don't let this happen and don't let others go down this path. Hold each other to the highest standards and be respectful in the process. When a project gets to 80 percent, raising it to 100 shouldn't take an inordinate amount of extra effort. The result will be happy customers, proud employees, and envious competitors.

Make each other the best. A coin has heads and tails. Courage is acting in the face of fear. Our value of integrity always also has a flipside, and making each other the best is it. Being constructively critical is essential. But we have to balance that by motivating each other and acknowledging success. When a large group of talented and driven individuals are all delivering quality work, there aren't many opportunities to formally acknowledge the highest achievers let alone everyone who deserves recognition. Everyone in the organization needs to take this on. Well-run startups have efficiency at their core, with all employees tackling more than most in larger organizations. The pace is incredible. So, it makes sense that only those who are moving at the same speed are in the best position to deliver praise and celebrate others' success. Another factor of this value is being inclusive and collaborative. The integrity of constructive debate and disagreement can only exist in conjunction with the act of bringing people and ideas together, teaching and learning from each other and offering to help and ask for help. Only in those environments can you respectfully challenge coworkers in order to benefit your company and therefore your customers. Related to these attributes is how your organization gives back to communities in need. Dedicating budget and people to goodwill endeavors is typically reserved for larger companies that have the resources. But employees can donate their time by attending events hosted by charity organizations that support the sick, elderly, homeless, and other often marginalized groups in our communities. Such efforts deliver impact to the recipients of that goodwill and to your employees. We get to see a different side of our coworkers while selflessly working side by side for our communities. By doing so, we create the relationships needed to comfortably praise and constructively challenge each other's work.

Get it done. Thinking big and delivering your absolute best each day emerge only when you actually deliver. Developing a great strategy is paramount. Executing on that strategy is even more crucial. It all starts with committing to what you're going to deliver and when. It's about following through from beginning to end. It's the accountability of making a promise and sticking to it. We've worked with people who use the terms, "I hope to ...," "The plan is to ...," "My goal is ...," and "If we ...." These are backdoors, hints that employees drop during group meetings or weekly 1:1 meetings with their managers. They are precursors to failure when a project is due or when multiple projects have been scheduled for delivery at the end of a quarter. Don't accommodate this behavior. Point it out immediately and let that person know you and others are there to help. They'll either raise their game or start looking for work at companies that don't operate at the speed of a startup. Either way, it's a win for the person and for your company. To achieve "get(ting) it done," everyone must subscribe to the adage of work hard and work smart. We've seen people who work a crazy amount of hours but are extremely unproductive. They're stressed, they constantly complain about their workload, and they miss deadlines and/or produce substandard work. They complain to their coworkers during meetings instead of staying on task. With complaining comes bad mouthing others. The last thing any coworker should do is acknowledge that person. It gives them the soap box they seek—that others are responsible for their own agony. In turn, they become convinced and justified about their views. At the same time, not everything goes as planned even for the most efficient and committed employees. You have to be agile, adjusting for all kinds of fires that a company experiences, and putting them out means putting on hold your committed deliverables. Those committed to getting it done expect these situations and find a path forward to accommodate both.

Own it. If you want your employees to deliver on their commitments, they first have to own those commitments. Many don't, and that will destroy a startup before it really gets started. Owning it means managing your commitments to the very end. It also means taking ownership for others. Yes, there are times when one employee is solely responsible for a failed project. More often than not, projects have multiple participants that include your peers and sometimes your business partners. That's why the business term "project owner" exists. There has to be one person who is not solely involved but ultimately responsible for an absolute best project that's completed on time. When something goes wrong, that person has to answer for it no matter who else is involved. Before that, they have to inform their manager of any project issues that they have tried to address more than once but were unsuccessful. That gives managers a heads-up about the project and an opportunity to step in, rectify the issues, and get the project moving in the right direction again and at the right pace. If the project owner fails to do so, no matter what the issue was or who else was responsible, that owner has to endure the consequences of failing to act. For Snowflake, owning it has another element. Anytime someone does make a mistake, they have to step up quickly, own the issues, and resolve them immediately. They must also view those situations positively and see the value in them. "What did I learn from that experience? How did I react? What did I learn about others involved? How will I avoid that from happening again? If a project does go wrong again, for any reason, will I be able to remain professional, take initiative, solve the problem, and move on?"

Embrace each other's differences. Before we can make each other their best, we have to accept them for who they are. As most startups do, Snowflake organized lunch for everyone most days of the week. At our San Mateo office, we would all squeeze into the largest space in our offices—an art deco kitchen area with a snow theme. Many of the tables were occupied by groups that originated from the same country. We have engineers who grew up in China, India, Germany, and Israel, and marketers from Sweden, Denmark, and Hungary. It was 2016, and there were maybe 75 of us working out of HQ. If there was an open seat anywhere, you grabbed it. At that moment, the conversation changed to one language so everyone could take part. We ate together and we shared stories about work and about life, no matter how different we were. When one of us was tapped to present at one of Bob Muglia's all-hands meetings, we all focused on that person. Marketers listened to engineers discuss coding projects and engineers learned about the next big marketing event that was coming. Everyone listened to what sales had to say. What truly united us was our shared mission. We were all committed to delivering the best. We wanted Snowflake to succeed beyond our own expectations. Snowflake was full of smart and humble professionals. We accepted and appreciated everyone from every walk of life and relied on our different strengths to move the needle.

Don't Just Write Them on a Wall

You should definitely write your company values on a wall, dedicate a page on your website, and have them readily available in your conference rooms. But you have to live them. Managers need to refer to them when meeting with their teams and during one-on-one's. They have to hold their employees accountable to your values. All goodwill efforts that employees do on behalf of Snowflake should have a dedicated page on your company website. On that page, the goodwill effort should tie back to one or more of your values. Departments should create quarterly awards focused on performance categories that tie back to your values. Allow everyone in the department to nominate their coworkers for each category. When you announce the winners, make a direct connection between how they performed in relation to that specific value. Choose an overall winner in each department who best represents all of your company's values. Depending on the size of your organization, you might consider choosing an overall winner for the entire company.

Review Your Values from Time to Time

A lot of time and effort should be part of developing your company's values. That also means you should review them once a year. Best to assemble a team assigned to this task and one that represents employees from different groups and with different backgrounds. Change it up every couple of years. As your company changes and expands, ask if your values still apply in all areas of the business. But don't feel you have to make serious changes to the values you first agreed on or add more values to your original list. Company values are similar to a country's enduring constitution. It might be amended from time to time but it shouldn't have to be rewritten. If the same unwanted behavior continues to emerge at your company, then the values could be a place to look. Or, it could just be one or two managers hiring the wrong people.

When People Don't Align with Your Values

Always keep your eyes and ears open to detect people or groups not living your company values. This could happen with individuals and teams geographically distant from your headquarters, between your employees and the partners in your business ecosystem, or a local manager who is attempting to cultivate a culture of bad behavior. This can happen early on with startups. It's crucial that a startup hires the best people for obvious reasons. That means they believe in your employees and your company values. For engineering, that wasn't too hard to accomplish. Our founders were well respected by their peers, and Mike Speiser was known for assembling solid engineering teams. For other areas of a company, hiring just one person that isn't a good fit can result in that person repeating that mistake. This can be disastrous for a small company. Solid professionals will question the organization they work for if people who won't align with its values keep getting hired. Eventually, the solid ones will leave. Don't let that happen. Best to remove all of those deemed as threats to your values, and do so at the same time. There's nothing worse for morale if you've identified those who have to go but remove one every couple of weeks. Before you do, be precise when evaluating the person or team identified. What's changed with them, when, and why? Is it their behavior or their performance? How did we miss this during the hiring process? We discuss this topic more in Chapter 11, looking at it from a wider context of hiring, retention, promotion, and parting ways. But it's also worth discussing in this chapter for early-stage startups to identify and rectify quickly.

Sales People, Culture, and Company Values

Of all the teams in an organization, sales seems to have the highest ratio of people who choose not to live a company's values. So there is merit in taking extra steps to ensure your values cascade down to every level of your sales organization. Most sales professionals tend to be highly permissive on a personal level. They don't always have the best ethics. They don't always do the best things in their personal lives. And the higher up in a sales organization, the more personally and professionally people have stretched morals. What's unique about Snowflake is that Bob is extremely ethical. Benoit and Thierry are good people. As Snowflake's sales and marketing leaders, we made it very clear early on how we should conduct ourselves, so we hired salespeople we thought could align with that. Sure, we hired gunslingers but not cowboys and definitely not scumbags. We hired people of good moral fiber. We didn't go out on the road and cheat on our spouses and go to strip clubs. We didn't go out and get drunk all night long and do drugs. And we didn't waste money on expense accounts. That made us highly focused on the mission and not on ancillary bullshit.

PHASE II
Build

7

Enter Marketing

"Chris, sales is my customer."

—Denise Persson

I GREW UP in Sweden. My father was a construction engineer, and my mother was a teacher. I didn't grow up with people talking business around the table. But education was important to them, and I'm grateful for that. My parents urged me to do well in school and go on to college to earn a business degree. But it was my only sibling, my sister, who exposed me to the business world at a young age. She is eight years my senior and began working in marketing and advertising while I was in high school. I often went to her office after school to do homework. She subscribed to *Resumé*—the Swedish marketing communications news magazine. Every week I rushed to her office to read the next edition. I read it from cover to cover, learning about the different campaigns companies relied on for their success. It drew me in and inspired me to become a career marketer.

After I graduated from Stockholm University, I joined the conferencing software company Genesys in 1996. My sister had a close friend who was a sales manager there and talked me into joining when it was just a startup. It was the mid-1990s and the highly coveted jobs back then in Sweden were at large companies. Joining a startup right out of college influenced my career heavily. I spent 12 years at Genesys, bouncing from Sweden to France and then eventually settling in the United States. During that time, I ascended to my ultimate role at the company as executive vice president of marketing. We invented then what Zoom is today. Genesys was acquired in 2008. Soon after, I joined the virtual communications software company ON24 as its CMO. I spent five years there and then occupied the same role at Apigee, an API platform company. I left Apigee in 2016, when Snowflake approached me.

When I interviewed with Chris, he asked me to reveal something about how others view me. I looked at him deadpanned and told him I was often referred to as the "Ice Queen" in my career. I was still locked in eye contact with him, paused, noticed he was stunned and then let him off the hook with my next statement: "Actually, people don't know that I'm pretty funny." We both smiled and laughed. What I am all about is going for it, delivering on decisions immediately, and bringing absolute impact to everything we do. I stay clear of esoteric discussions, I challenge vague promises, and I keep conversations in the trees, not the weeds. No one slips anything past me, especially in a group meeting. I will challenge them when I sniff a strategy that isn't one or when its execution is half-baked. I'm upfront but purposeful, so everyone else listening or watching knows not to repeat what they just witnessed. The first people I hired inspired those who came later. They had worked for me previously, so they copped twice as much because they knew better and they bounced back immediately. My gaze isn't narrow. I treat vendors the same. We pay them a lot of money based on commitments they make to gain our business. When they don't deliver, and it happens sometimes, I let them know why and what's at stake for our customers and our company.

Your CMO

A lot of CMOs have big egos. They know how good they are at what they do. Hire someone who has bragging rights but doesn't brag. They must be humble, for at least three reasons. Most days they will work very closely with the founders and executive management. Chest beating isn't well received when those on the other end of that behavior are humble and brilliant. And egomaniacs tend to hire people like themselves or hire a bunch of door mats—neither of which will fit your company's culture and values. Your CMO must also work in lockstep with sales and must be willing to work as an individual contributor in the beginning, while trying to hire their first few key marketers. Rolling up your sleeves early on in your tenure as a CMO is a must and gains a lot of respect. But if that person continues to work heavily as an individual contributor after they hire a team, and not pass those responsibilities to their subordinates, that too is a cause for concern. When they're not engaging their peers, they have to manage their team with impact. They must focus on driving measurable results with every strategy, program, and execution. This mindset must cascade down to every layer of management and to every individual contributor. If it can't be measured, then it won't deliver impact.

No two CMOs approach marketing the same way. We all manage a number of distinctly different functions. Yet, we each have our own mission that defines how all of those functions operate alongside one another and toward that mission. What makes sense for one marketing organization during a specific phase of a company may not work for others. Snowflake hired me for a number of reasons, including the promise I made to Chris that marketing would serve sales if I was at the helm. They desperately needed to increase their trickle of leads to a constant flow, so our sales team could establish Snowflake as a viable competitor in a tech sector owned by 8,000 lb rhinos, young and old. Revenue can't grow without sales doing its job. Sales can't do its job without an abundant amount of qualified leads. Sales doesn't have the time to generate all of their leads, but marketing should.

Assessing Marketing Incumbents

The first thing I had to tackle was building the team and figuring out how we were going to establish credibility for Snowflake. We were going to compete against some of the largest companies on the planet. At the same time, we had to convince customers to put their most valuable asset, their data, into Snowflake. My job was to come in and build the team. In particular, build the demand generation function with other marketing functions supporting it.

Back in 2016, Snowflake had just over 100 people, which still comprised mainly engineers and sales professionals, and a few finance and customer support people. But the company had also hired seven marketers prior to my arrival. The person who led the team when I arrived was very intelligent and incredibly talented, but they came from a product background, with limited experience building functions such as demand generation. That couldn't work if sales and marketing were going to be successful and absolutely aligned with each other. There was also friction between sales and marketing when I came on board. It was a culture of conflict. I fired two marketers within a couple of months. Over the next couple of years, we let another few of them go for various reasons. Looking back, they should have departed Snowflake sooner than they did. They were good people but either in the wrong role, at the wrong company, at the wrong time, or a combination of all three. How that showed up each day was how they aligned themselves with our company values and our sales team.

Chris was Snowflake's first sales rep, so he had to be careful about who he hired in the early days and going forward. I had to be similarly vigilant. I also had to assess the people in marketing who arrived before me. If they didn't align with our values, then keeping them on the team would be similar to hiring someone new with that same disposition. I also had to show the company that I was willing to tackle issues head on, and immediately, no matter how sensitive they might be and even if the departing employees started long before I arrived.

I needed to shift the focus of the team to realize that we are here to help the sales folks sell. That's our job. Not to tell sales what to do. We had to give more to the other side before they would reciprocate. That's how you get trust from sales. You can't come in and demand trust. Trust is built. It took about six months to accomplish this. By then, the leads were coming in and the sales reps were generating deals from those leads.

Your First Hires

I needed to hire, and fast. I chose people who had a lot of experience, could wear many hats, and who had no problem with rolling up their sleeves as individual contributors until they would hire and manage their own teams. They had all worked for me previously or I knew a lot about them through previous experiences. Reason being, hiring is such a gamble. You may not know for six months whether or not that person is going to work out. The more senior the person, the longer that evaluation can take. In addition to their versatility, they had to be entrepreneurs in their own domains and have that same spirit when collaborating with others. They had to know their craft, be self-starters, and be ready to huddle with no notice. They had to come up with great marketing ideas on the fly that would grab prospects' attention and leave a lasting impression. They also had to be committed to the Snowflake cause, meaning, they believed in Snowflake to such a degree they would remain for at least five years or when Snowflake failed, whichever came first. And they had to know people—people whom they wanted to be their first hires. Contractors were also a big part of our efforts early on. We also needed the help of small agencies that specialized in specific areas of marketing that could do the work because we didn't have the headcount yet for those functions. Of course, new hires had to believe in our company values and would live them every day.

At other companies, too often I see people pointing fingers at each other, shuffling PowerPoint presentations from one department over to another. There's little execution taking place. When we're trying to hit a triple, triple, triple, double, double, in terms of revenue, year over year, you need execution. As Frank Slootman, one of our previous CEOs, said: "Your strategy is only as good as your execution." Otherwise, your strategy will sit on a shelf somewhere if you can't translate it into actionable deliverables. All of my first hires dedicated at least seven years to Snowflake and counting. All but one were still working at Snowflake as this book took shape.

Demand Generation

Chris was generating the leads, but they were trickling in and there was no machine in place to ramp that up. He told John McMahon, "I'm nervous that I don't have a partner on the other side who understands demand generation." The CMO is someone who has to generate sales leads. It's the number one most important thing a company in growth mode can do. You can have a mediocre product but market the hell out of it and still make money. But even the best technology in the world won't sell if your demand gen is substandard. If you don't have leads, you're dead.

Of all the marketing functions, demand gen is the one that flies closest to sales. I devoted big resources to that and had a strong sense of what good looked like based on my time leading other marketing organizations. Snowflake was starting to gain traction. Chris wanted a genuine partner he could work with and a marketing team that would align with sales to bring in potential customers. He was under pressure from the board to scale the sales organization, and demand gen was an essential enabler of that.

Establishing a productive and effective demand gen operation, and everything it needed from other marketing teams, was my mission when I arrived at Snowflake. We had to increase the outputs of that function almost exponentially. Lars Christensen had led demand gen teams for a number of tech companies and did so when he worked for me at ON24. He was already a tech veteran when I contacted him within days after I joined Snowflake. He had the experience, insights, and humility that were vital to jump-starting a world class demand gen organization. Lars focused on a few key initiatives to get things rolling that a company should expect from its head of demand gen.

1. As an individual contributor, increase the flow of leads, while liaising with sales management on an almost daily basis.
2. Contract with small marketing consulting firms to execute aspects of demand generation until the team is large enough to bring those functions in house.
3. Hire proven experts from different functional areas of demand gen, who had worked for him previously and who could be individual contributors before they built out their own teams.
4. Deploy the apps and marketing operations needed to automate nearly every process of demand gen, and to track the impact marketing campaigns had on advancing prospects through the sales funnel.
5. Partner with a content marketing leader to develop value-based content and messaging that would address the top challenges faced by Snowflake's targeted personas.

When Lars first arrived, everything at Snowflake was ad hoc. Lars and I approached demand gen in terms of repeatability and predictability. When you align yourself with sales, you can't just show up once a month and say, "Hey, we were at a trade show, and now we have 300 leads for you." Then, nothing more happens for the next three weeks until you send out the next email, when you might get another 150 leads. As the leads flow in, they roll to each sales territory. The sales team can get snowed under with too many leads at a single point in time. You must create a pipeline with a steady flow of leads so reps can work on them each day in a very predictable way. We wanted to stimulate demand, not in waves, but in a constant flow.

With demand, it's about using many channels, digital advertising, and optimizing and building up our own database. Our team would target our personas en masse and also conduct targeted campaigns by mapping out a big enterprise prospect, identifying the key individuals and educating them. We targeted them with offers via social media. It's all about how we engage people in that account. It's also about timing the value prop with a prospect's need. It could be up to 15 touchpoints to engage them and then we follow up and eventually hand the lead over to the sales team. Making a salesperson find the right people in an account is not where they should focus, but marketing can do that at scale.

Content Marketing

A solid demand gen machine requires a great deal of value-driven content. Without it, you might as well own a Ferrari a thousand miles from the nearest gas station. Messaging and content are crucial to how a startup positions itself to customers, the market, and the investment community. The genesis of your content strategy isn't about delivering a bunch of white papers, ebooks, and product briefs. It helps drive all of your marketing in those early days. Product, customer, and field marketing all need content and public relations, as well. Tight budgets and absolute brand continuity from day one demand that your content strategy and execution are in lock step with all of marketing. But there's something more. You need a company-wide editorial process, plain and simple, and it has to start at the very beginning. Otherwise, your customers and prospects will get the same brand experience they get from most other startups and large companies—mediocre and conflicting content, and disjointed messaging from multiple fiefdoms operating independent of one another.

I hired Vince Morello to lead content because marketing today is about education. I called him at 9 am on my first day at Snowflake. He and I met a year before while I was CMO at Apigee. He didn't take the job we offered him then but joined Snowflake six weeks after I did. I sought him out because he had worked in demand gen and later in sales at Oracle, a soon-to-be Snowflake competitor. He later retrained to become a news and investigative journalist. He was my first hire as Lars needed a few months to exit his role at his previous company. Sales and journalism made Vince a highly competitive person when it came to content. His mantra is to always grab readers with the first three words, provide a fresh angle, and then deliver value throughout every piece of content. He observed that very few tech firms accomplish this. To do so at Snowflake, he deployed the art of storytelling, in everything from a short banner ad on social media to an 80-page booklet about data warehouses.

He was originally tasked with jump-starting Snowflake's content marketing, which is not about traditional product marketing. It's the phase at the very top of the sales funnel—content designed to provide insights into your prospects' problems without pushing your products or services. You become more their partner than a vendor. They begin to rely on your content and then develop a curiosity about what you do offer in the way of solutions. As they move further down the funnel, you expose them to more traditional content about your products and services before they eventually make contact with a sales rep.

Vince produced the content offered in our demand generation campaigns, but he also wrote the emails, web landing pages, and banner ads that enabled those campaigns. He developed our press releases and content for our product, customer, and field marketing functions. He produced content across all mediums—digital, web, print, video, and audio. He was the only writer and editor in marketing at the time, and he took the same approach for those traditional forms of marketing as he did with content and thought leadership marketing. As a journalist, he had interviewed thousands of people, so he worked well with our engineers, and our sales reps and sales engineers, to understand everything about the product and about the customer pain points Snowflake could solve. He once adapted a slide deck from one of our sales engineers and turned it into an ebook. It performed incredibly well. Like a journalist, there were no boundaries when it came to generating ideas for content. As a former salesperson, he saw the value of minimizing direct contact between sales reps and prospects early in the sales cycle. He produced content that addressed questions prospects often had during that phase, so our sales reps could focus on opportunities further down the funnel. This streamlined things for our sales team, helping them scale their operations outside of hiring more reps. Vince spent seven years at Snowflake, with his last three years as our chief storyteller.

Marketing is about promoting great educational content and spending time with sales reps to make sure content always addresses the things prospects want to learn about. Every Friday, Vince sat down with sales engineers to learn about the conversations they had that week with prospects. This helped him understand how to position Snowflake to address their technical and business challenges around data and how to advance their data strategies overall. No one else had that content, so people would come to Snowflake to learn. Not enough marketers really execute on that. Putting ourselves in their world, not the other way around.

Kicking off your content strategy early in your startup stage is vital to all areas of marketing. You need someone who can write incredibly well, and fast. That means they will hire those who can meet that same level of quality and speed as you expand your content operations. In all of your marketing teams, you need an edge. For content, it was our journalism style of writing and our newsroom style of envisioning and producing content. You also have to prepare yourself for the resistance from marketers who later join the team. Product marketers, like many others in your marketing organization, consider themselves to be writers and will draft a product brief or white paper, edit and proofread it themselves, and then send it to a graphic designer. Marketers aren't writers but they know the product area they oversee very well. So, they should be involved from the very beginning, but they can't be the only person. They have to conform with the editorial process that you establish. Some will resist at first but most will be patient long enough to see the benefits. Others, well, they end up having to depart your organization.

Customer Marketing

Early on, we already had happy customers. Because they were so delighted with the product, they were happy to talk about it. Eszter Szikora worked for me at Apigee as head of social media and marketing communications. She was my third hire at Snowflake. She jumpstarted our customer marketing and was given public relations and other teams to manage as the marketing organization continued to grow. Eszter is the manifestation of relentlessness with a smile. In the early days, Eszter built strong relationships with many of our customers and got them involved in our marketing. She didn't promote them like other tech companies did—showcasing them like they were prized ponies in the Snowflake stable. Instead, she had them speak for us.

She produced dozens of short, sharp, and simple customer videos. This accomplished a few things. First and foremost was our tight budget. We didn't have the money to do big video productions around our customers. Secondly, Snowflake didn't have any big-name customers. Even our first few big-name customers wouldn't do any marketing with us. They viewed becoming a customer of such a small company as a risk they could handle. But appearing in our marketing programs was something else entirely. For our smaller customers, we developed a short list of questions to get each interview started and then let things roll from there. It was just Eszter and a single videographer with a tripod and camera, and Vince helped out from a storytelling perspective. Because our product comprised about 10 or so technology areas, she got customers to talk about which of those areas were most important to their organizations and how Snowflake was uniquely different from our competitors. From there, our customers discussed the business benefits of Snowflake, such as ease of use and greater access to more data and insights than competing products offered.

That first wave of interviews was done so simply. They happened during our customer advisory meetings at local, mid-range hotels. We would ask one of them to step out for 10 minutes for an interview. The customer sat on a stool in front of the camera in a small hotel conference room. We once hosted a happy hour for these customers in the kitchen area of our small office space. Sure enough, one by one, we would politely usher them across the hall into our conference room where we were ready to film. With a target of just two minutes per video after editing, we moved customers through each interview quickly, extracting all of the vital points and surrounded by their passion for their jobs and how Snowflake made their jobs so much easier. We had to get the videos approved by each of our customers' legal teams, but that never prevented us from politely capitalizing on having so many happy customers in one place at the same time.

The same strategy happened with our live events. Bob would deliver a passionate keynote, creating clear delineations between our technology and that of our competitors. Sometime later in that one-day event, we would get four or five customers sitting on stage together. We had our own moderator ask a few questions to get the conversation rolling. Then we let the panel take over the conversation, inspiring prospects in the audience to ask question after question. A lot of those questions were in response to the disbelief of what they heard. Snowflake was almost too good to be true, and they needed a customer to confirm it for them.

We did not have a vertical marketing strategy, segmenting customers by industry. That came later. As a small company, we were simply focusing on the technical benefits of Snowflake and what it meant to store and manage their data more easily and comprehensively, and extract insights from that data. This approach made sense for the first couple of years of marketing. But our method of delivering those messages was first and foremost through our customers. We made them happy because of our technology, and we treated them well during the relationship. And that strategy remained as the marketing team grew. Data warehousing became one of a number of data workloads Snowflake could handle, and we eventually verticalized our go-to-market strategy. As a startup it can be time-consuming to manage a customer marketing program when you have limited resources, but it's worth every minute. Second to our initial public offering (IPO), I can attribute nearly 100 percent of our brand awareness to customer advocacy.

Field Marketing

Field sales reps are as critical and impatient as they are driven. They know how important their jobs are to a company, so when they call on someone from outside their organization for help, they *really* need it.

If you don't respond immediately or respond but fail to deliver value, then they will dismiss you and your organization. Why? Because they need to focus on developing opportunities and closing business with urgency. When marketing takes the initiative, continues to deliver more than what a field sales rep expects, and delights them in the process, you've cemented a relationship that traverses a path from the bottom up. That can be more effective than a sales-marketing relationship that starts with your executive management but often fizzles somewhere down the line.

Caitlin Griffith DeMartini started at Snowflake just a month before I did but as a sales development rep (SDR) with Chris's team at our San Mateo office. It was her first and only sales job, and she was successful in that role for her first six months. But I saw even bigger potential for her in field marketing and politely stole her from Chris. Even a short time in such a small sales organization, which was moving very quickly, exposed her to working relationships with most of Snowflake's field sales reps. They already knew her, so gaining their trust was easier than if she was a new hire or someone who had no sales experience.

Caitlin got to work quickly to understand each sales rep's needs in terms of lead generation and the types of events each rep or region needed. At this early stage, we didn't have a repeatable or scalable event that we could host around the country—or the world, for that matter. We didn't need one. We had a few dozen reps, so we hosted small events at cool venues such as microbreweries and the like. The reps chose the prospects and customers they wanted to invite. Caitlin suggested venues and worked with each rep to create an agenda and secure speakers for brief talks during these events. One of the key ways that we measure our field marketing programs is through the pipeline dollar value that a program touches. When you're looking at customer progression in a sales funnel, you have different digital vehicles out there (mainly content) reaching prospects via different touch points. Field marketing really kicks in after customers enter the sales cycle. At our smaller hospitality events and highly targeted field events, we typically attract attendees who are already well into the sales cycle. They are not new prospects. It's just too expensive to use those events that way, at that level. They are part of a pipeline acceleration strategy. Many times, we will attract those prospects and a number of their colleagues, who have a say or a stake in their organization choosing Snowflake. When this happens, it's a telltale sign they are close to making a purchase decision.

Partner Marketing

Saqib Mustafa is what we call a "true believer." He was working for Teradata—a long-time data warehouse competitor that started more than 30 years before Snowflake's founders and engineers typed their first line of code. Teradata created an all-in-one "appliance" that included on-premises hardware and data warehousing software. Later on, Teradata offered a cloud version of its solution. Saqib had a computer science degree and was working in pre-sales at Teradata when he heard about Snowflake. After a closer look at what Snowflake was about, he was hooked and joined the product marketing team a few months before I arrived. There was someone in charge of partner marketing when I arrived, but the role was not a good fit for that person. So, I moved Saqib into that role. His job was to work closely with product marketing and Snowflake's alliance team to develop marketing strategies with our growing group of technology partners.

If we deliver marketing events on our own, it's a lot of work to get people to come. But if we host a live event with two of our partners, we will all invite our customers and prospects. We're going to get three times the reach compared to going it alone. We also did webinars, display advertising, and content marketing together. And even though we positioned Snowflake bigger than a startup, we always piggybacked on the credibility of much larger partners. Budgets weren't incredibly tight, but you have to be very smart with the money you have.

Joint marketing programs cement a clear and consistent message to convey to your target audiences. Many startups strike partnerships with other technology companies and promote those relationships on their websites. That's not easy but it's the easiest part of a go-to-market strategy with partners. The true challenge is messaging around that partnership—how each of your products works, how the technologies integrate, the value customers receive, and how that integration and value from that partnership differ from a competitor's relationships with other partners that market a similar joint solution.

Only during a content strategy session, do you realize all of this. Otherwise, if you skip this part, all you're doing is placing your product messaging next to theirs. This is lazy marketing, and your prospects will see that for what it is.

You can't market with all your partners. We first cemented our relationships with the cloud infrastructure providers, the ETL and ELT technology companies, and the business intelligence solution providers. These complementary technologies were essential to hosting Snowflake in the cloud, getting data into Snowflake, and getting insights out of Snowflake. Following that, we struck relationships with all kinds of technology and service providers. We needed them all, but we could only invest a great deal of time and money with partners that we often joined forces with in sales opportunities. One or two joint opportunities in a year doesn't justify joint marketing with a partner. Closing dozens or even hundreds of joint deals with a single partner each year does.

Account-Based Marketing (ABM)

ABM is integral to sales and is one of the marketing functions that helps enable absolute alignment between sales and marketing. But how does it work? At Snowflake, we jump-started this team when we created our first named account team within our sales organization. As we grew from hundreds of customers to thousands, we scaled our ABM strategy to align with our goals to grow our named account customer base. We started by deploying a multi-level strategy by aligning our ABM people with named account sales reps. Later, we aligned ABM with our sales development reps (SDRs), who advance leads to a point where sales reps can justifiably make contact with those prospects.

> **Tier 1:** Our regional sales vice presidents identify up to five prospect accounts each that they see as having significant deal-size potential. These are huge organizations that could generate a multitude of sales opportunities. They have many use cases that span departments, subsidiaries, and geographic regions and could benefit from deploying our product. We create events, custom emails, advertising, microsites, and other forms of one-to-one custom content. The topics focus

on the prospects' technical and business pain points, the topics of interest they share with our sales reps, and the challenges they often encounter specific to their vertical industry. We also leverage SaaS products that capture intent data to reveal the topics the people in these accounts are researching. The cross-functional team you assemble and assign to execute your ABM strategy for each of these accounts should include someone from ABM, sales development, field marketing, partner marketing, and field sales.

Tier 2: Have your account executives in field sales identify between five to seven prospect accounts that would be strategic to their sales pipeline. Then deploy a one-to-few approach with custom ads for each group, a microsite they can visit that features existing but curated content and events, personal outreach from your field sales rep, and tailored outreach from your SDRs. Invite these prospects to field marketing events with their region and include content about your product and services that can help address their technical and business challenges. Assemble a cross-functional team similar to your tier one approach. But because this is a one-to-few strategy, swap out your ABM person for folks from your demand generation team.

Tier 3: This is also a one-to-few approach, but based on intent activity within a specific region and led by your ABM managers, district sales managers, and SDRs. This cross-functional team identifies top themes within a geographic region and uses intent data to choose three to five accounts in a region that are actively researching those themes. From there, create engagement, establish first meetings, and reveal new opportunities in these prospect accounts. Your programs for these accounts should take advantage of the alignment and scale you continue to develop across and between marketing and sales. Your ABM team can launch targeted ads that point to a microsite focused on a region or theme. Build this personalized microsite to turn visitor insights into page customizations upon page load. This is not a one-to-many approach that offers the same experience to all accounts within a single segment. Instead, it allows you to deliver a one-to-one ABM experience at scale.

Overall, use your ABM strategy to land and expand new accounts and to expand existing accounts. Many accounts that qualify for an ABM strategy will become strategic to your sales strategy as they come to trust your company and rely on your product and insights. At the very top, a single named account can be the only account a field sales rep maintains. Some of these individual accounts require more than one sales rep, because the amount of business they do with you is significant. Yet, with all of the benefits that a well-run ABM strategy delivers, your demand gen team still plays a significant role developing awareness and interest in your named accounts. Both ABM and demand generation focus on understanding the needs of different industries and sub-industries, and the pain points of prospective buyers, by delivering personalized marketing messaging and sales efforts.

Public Relations

PR firms are limited because their clients are spread across a number of industries. Even if a firm has a tech focus, their clients could span dozens of different tech sectors. We were impressed with each one we chose. Their people and presentations were always solid but none of them understood the depth of our technology, how it differed from our competitors, or what it would require from a PR firm to help achieve our overall company strategy. We couldn't expect them to. We had so much to tell the public about our product and we were the best at doing so. We also faced challenges that many startups have to endure. Our competitors wrongly stated what our product was capable of or how our product compared to theirs. Journalists had good intentions, but similar to the PR firms we used, didn't always accurately explain what our product offered. Once we developed a robust PR strategy and hired enough people, we moved nearly all of that function in-house at Snowflake.

We added PR to Eszter's responsibilities. She had more than 10 years of marketing communications experience at companies prior to joining Snowflake. She got to work quickly, expanding her team globally in lockstep with Snowflake's expansion due to customer demand in Europe, Asia, and Australia. She also coordinated all of our PR employees, contractors, and vendors across the globe, so they were in sync with worldwide product announcements and events. It was not long before we brought most of the PR strategy and execution inside Snowflake. PR firms have their place but just be sure that you're getting the value for what these firms charge. You won't really need one when you're still developing your product. When you're nearing GA, or when you've started marketing via other channels, employing a PR firm makes sense. Just set your expectations correctly about how far they can help you and what you should pay them based on the services they actually provide your company.

What Matters

We hired great people, but still we deployed a quarterly results system to hold each marketer accountable. We titled it, "What Matters in Marketing." Each person in marketing works with their manager to develop a short list of the most important projects they planned to complete in every financial quarter, and the measurable results they would have to attain to show their success. We often call these the huge "rocks" we plan to move. For the demand gen folks, it would be the number of programs they completed, how many campaign responses we received, the engagement created within a targeted named account, prospects who attended our live or online events, and how many qualified prospect meetings they generated. For public relations, it's about the PR calendar of events, how they promote them, and the measurable response they created. It also relates to how many original articles about Snowflake that PR gets placed in industry publications or how many times Snowflake is mentioned in articles written by journalists about our industry. It goes this way for everyone in marketing. At the end of each quarter, each marketer reports on what they achieved against their stated goals from three months before. Their performance, or lack thereof, determines how much of their quarterly bonus they receive. Minor projects or daily activities do not make a person's What Matters list. Anything that resembles a statement from a job description doesn't make the list either. Those are broad responsibilities that can't be measured, and to which you can't hold people accountable.

8

The Five Pillars of Marketing

"If the foundation is not strong, the walls will creak."

—Denise Persson

As a startup's head of marketing, you have to put a stake in the ground. You're hustling all day every day to deliver immediate impact, while trying to hire people and assess the marketers who have arrived before you. You're also creating strong relationships with sales, engineering, and other teams, while addressing the requests these teams have stockpiled in anticipation of your arrival. With all that swirling around, you also must create a fundamental context that determines every marketing decision. Without alignment within marketing, alignment with other teams will never happen.

Market positioning is the foundation of everything you do. You need to get that right from the beginning. If you start doing marketing without first establishing your position in the market you risk constantly changing your messaging and nothing will stick. As you help build a company, you're building mindshare. With mindshare, you need extreme consistency. If I've learned anything from previous companies, the wind changes direction every day and companies feel they need to change their position and messaging too. By doing so, you accomplish nothing. People don't know what you stand for.

One of the first things I did when I arrived at Snowflake was to create our five pillars of marketing. This came from my experience prior to Snowflake, helping take three companies public. Snowflake had about 100 employees, and we were marketing and competing against the biggest vendors in the tech industry. How should we go to market? How should we engage prospects and customers? How were we going to win? That's how our pillars of marketing emerged. We developed them to answer those questions and others. We created them in 2016, and we still rely on them today.

The Pillars

Pillar 1—Define Your Market Position

With clear, targeted, and verified positioning, the marketing programs you create will be far stronger and more effective. There are many ways to define positioning. The one I always refer to comes from the book *Positioning*, by Al Ries, published more than 20 years ago. Ries describes positioning as the battle for your prospect's mind. And winning the battle is all about how well you differentiate yourself. When you are a startup, you only have a few seconds to explain what you do. So you can't overcomplicate your positioning. Startups often focus on categories that take too long to explain. Time is not your friend in those early days. Your positioning needs to be incredibly relevant, as well. Most startups do a handful of interviews with current customers who already know you, but that isn't enough. You need data and insights from prospects, so you can determine if your positioning will work with the broader market, not just your early adopters. This kind of data-driven process also makes it much easier to get buy-in from everyone in your company.

The most successful brands in the world are also the most consistent brands. Consistency builds trust, and people buy from brands they trust. Therefore employees, partners, and customers all need to describe you in the same way. We worked with a Silicon Valley firm to determine our product differentiation and how to position that to prospects and our total addressable market. Don't attempt this from within your company. It's an involved and exhaustive process that a startup is not staffed to handle. Moreover, you need professionals who have done this exercise with many companies over the years. They also have fresh eyes, which challenges the preconceived views from even the most gifted people in your startup of what the outcomes should be. That's a good thing. Our goal was to empower Snowflake to tell a consistent story across all touchpoints based on input from Snowflake's leadership team, customers, analysts, partners, and prospects. Briefly, here are the top-line, key positioning elements that emerged from this exercise:

- **Our market category** was the "Data warehouse built for the cloud." This was important for two reasons: It placed us into a well-known product category, data warehousing, established decades before Snowflake was founded. Prospects already had a data warehouse or a budget line item to buy or replace such a solution. So, we've hitched ourselves to a large market and avoided the Herculean effort of trying to establish and market a brand-new product category. We were in constant panhandling mode with venture capitalists for continued funding that could run out at any time. Again, time was not on our side. But what we offered the market was much more than the data warehouse incumbents.
- **What made us different** to this market was "built for the cloud." We chose those four words very carefully, and the order in which they appear. Our solution was not just for the cloud, but built for the cloud, which is something vastly different once explained in greater detail. It wasn't entirely clear to our audience yet, but that's all we needed this high up in our messaging. We weren't being abstract and we weren't waffling on. Most tech companies position themselves at one of these two extremes this early with their messaging. We were simply piquing prospects' interest so they would keep inquiring.
- The next element of our message was to detail **our promise and make good on that promise.** Many companies accomplish the first part but not the second. In essence, they accomplish nothing. Worse, they disillusion prospects. We achieved both with three simple defining characteristics from which we could easily provide more detail:

- **Performance:** Experience multi-petabyte scale, with up to 200× faster performance compared to your existing solution.
- **Concurrency:** Enable a near-infinite amount of people and processes to access a single copy of your data simultaneously with no impact to performance.
- **Simplicity:** Deploy a fully managed solution with a pay-as-you-go business model and accommodate all of your structured and semi-structured data.

Other elements we defined with this exercise were the market opportunity, the problem Snowflake wanted to solve, and our tagline, vision, and mission statements. We relied on this messaging for the next two to three years, when it became obvious Snowflake was more than just a data warehouse built for the cloud. When that happened, we commenced a slimmed-down version of this exercise with the same Silicon Valley marketing firm. We were able to do so because we did not need to revisit some of the work in the first version of establishing our market position. It's best to revisit your overall position every two to three years in the early stages of a startup. Even if your product doesn't change, your competitors' products will. More importantly, your market is always changing. Events associated with data security and new technologies such as generative AI were just two of many reasons to review our brand sooner rather than later.

Pillar 2—Be the Most Customer-Centric Marketing Team in Your Industry

The most admired brands in the world have at least three things in common. They own their categories, they are all incredibly consistent with their brand experience, and they have incredible customer loyalty. At Snowflake, we put the customer first. We position that company value first on our website, for a reason. We were determined to create the most customer-centric marketing team in the software industry. To do that, you have to look from the outside in every day. And you need to take the pulse of your customers' needs all the time. Your absolute focus has to be genuinely helping customers. This is really what marketing is about. Research what their needs and challenges are, because no amount of content about your product will help solve those issues when you're wide of the mark with an inside-out approach to marketing. As a start-up, you don't have to spend a lot of money to accomplish this. Chris Degnan was doing this from day one, by providing feedback from potential customers to our engineers who were still developing our product. Sure, this culminated in new product features, but those features were added to solve the data problems of prospective customers.

Later on, Snowflake created a product management team to prioritize the development of new features and functionality. Our product marketers worked with that team to develop a detailed persona for every type of potential customer influencer, at all levels and across all technical domains. It was quite a task but had every characteristic we needed to pinpoint each persona with the right messages from all of our marketing channels. The personas included age range, level, and type of education, years of experience, title, responsibilities, level of influence over the purchase of a software solution, and the pain points they would continue to endure until they ran their business with Snowflake.

Once you amass a bunch of customers, develop ways to get constant customer feedback. Start an annual customer engagement survey as early as possible. At Snowflake, we used an external firm to help us measure every single component of the Snowflake customer experience. From this annual survey, we also obtained our net promoter score (NPS). An NPS is the result of surveying your customers about how likely they are to recommend your product to others. On a scale of 1 to 10, those customers who rank a vendor from 0 to 6 are detractors. Those who rank you from 7 to 8 are passives. And those who rank you from 9 to 10 are promoters. Your NPS is then calculated by subtracting the detractors from the promoters and disregarding the passives. A score of 30–40 in the technology industry is considered average. Anything 70 or higher is exceptional. Snowflake has produced scores just above or just below 70 since we first started measuring our NPS. But we don't conduct this survey to show how well we're doing. We do so to find out which customers aren't completely satisfied with Snowflake and address those issues.

We eventually established a Customer Success team to further enhance our focus on customers. But it didn't last long. Frank Slootman surprised us when he arrived in 2019 as Snowflake's second CEO.

He shut it down and absorbed the team into other groups within the company. He believed that customer success should not rest with one single team in a company. If so, how effective can one team be for hundreds, thousands, or even tens of thousands of customers you must serve? And how is one team able to bring everything to its customers that its company has to offer? Sales, marketing, alliances, finance, support, and engineering all touch the customer. Some teams more than others. Frank's belief was that every single employee should put its customers at the center of everything they do.

As a startup, as soon as you have actual customers, do everything you possibly can to put them at the forefront of your marketing. At Snowflake, we have a rule that all of our marketing programs should always feature a customer. Customers are by far your most effective marketing tool. Prospects simply trust their peers more than they trust you.

Pillar 3—Build for Automation and Scale Early On

One big problem many startups encounter is that they reach $20 million in revenue relatively quickly. Then, their growth slows, because they rely too much on manual work. Our motto in marketing, and across the rest of Snowflake, has always been to "automate everything." In 2017, the big topic at Snowflake all-hands meetings centered on automation—getting rid of "the hamsters." The hamsters were real people doing work that should be handled by a software application either purchased or built by Snowflake, for Snowflake. We even had someone dress up as a hamster in a wheel for our Halloween party that year. Having hamsters in the very beginning made sense for Snowflake. There were so few people that it didn't make sense to automate processes that you don't yet have the infrastructure to implement. But you will realize very soon, as a startup, you can't scale a company with hamsters.

Before you start blowing cash on software you're not ready to use, identify the three types of marketing automation you may need. The first is out of necessity. Otherwise, you can't do your jobs. To start, deploy a customer relationship management (CRM) platform and a marketing automation platform (MAP). Chris started using a CRM product when he first arrived at Snowflake. Those working in marketing from the very beginning used a MAP solution that we continued to run for lead generation programs. In both of these situations, you're automating a process that hasn't been done manually for decades. Using software is the only sensible option no matter how many people are in a company. There is nothing to phase out here as these products enable you to scale an operation before you need additional people.

The second type of automation is when you're already using software, but these solutions require you to manually enter and extract data you need. Spreadsheets, word processing programs, and legacy database products are examples of solutions with elements of both manual and automated processes. They need to be phased out, or avoided altogether, so teams don't become reliant on them to run their operations. The barriers to developing open, versatile, and user-friendly applications are so low these days that a number of competing SaaS applications exist to automate almost any business process. If you have to start replacing things in the midst of all the great momentum you're building, it's going to slow you down. It's all about moving sooner and faster than anybody else.

The third form of automating with software involves processes that can't exist without a software solution. In essence, if you aren't using a SaaS product, then that process doesn't exist. This is where Snowflake's marketing team focused and this is how we scaled with automation. We started with 1, then 3, then 8, and eventually we subscribed to more than 30 SaaS products for our marketing stack. These are solutions that allow us to conceive and deploy the most elegant, targeted, and impactful market programs, while capturing and analyzing every action made by prospects known and unknown to us. Along the way, we created a marketing operations team to review, approve, deploy, and support each app. We required every marketer to follow this process when selecting software for data security and other purposes. Otherwise, every team within marketing that has a budget can subscribe to any SaaS product without oversight. Most organizations continue to endure this type of "application sprawl," which becomes a nightmare for their IT department and makes it impossible to centralize all of your data in order to conduct the most advanced marketing analytics.

Lars Christensen and his team made sure every component of our demand generation process could be automated and scaled. They also automated things (without AI) you wouldn't think could be automated. Any company of any size can relate to the enormous number of requests for customer references it receives. The demand gen team transformed this traditionally manual process when they introduced a weekly office hour during which prospects could ask questions of a customer in a live, non-scripted way about anything related to our product. This was not a traditional customer reference call, but it replaced that method with a forum-like environment in which many prospects could get their questions answered and listen to questions posed by their peers. This scalable, hands-off approach saved the marketing and sales teams enormous amounts of time that we could spend on other things, and it meant we didn't have to annoy customers every time a prospect thought it needed a 1:1 reference call.

Today, we still drive our prospects to a weekly office hour. No question is off-limits. Our office hours have grown rapidly, and we now have hundreds of prospects attending them each day. We've done the same with our local workshops. Initially, we conducted them out in the field. But long before the COVID-19 pandemic, we moved them online. The online versions perform much better. To get your company to $100 million in revenue and much further, you need to get rid of the hamsters as soon as you can. When you're rapidly scaling, you have to look at every component of your buyer's journey and replace everything you can that is time-consuming, with procedures that are automated and replicable.

Pillar 4—Be Bold

To break through, you have to be noticed, and the challenge is that building brand awareness takes time, especially for a small company. Startups don't have millions to pour into traditional advertising, and Snowflake was competing with the largest and most well-known brands in the world. So what do you do? What are your options? You have to be bold from the beginning. Being bold is not without risk, and not every management team is up for it. At Snowflake, our vision of being bold fit with our values. Our inspiration came from Virgin America, which disrupted the airline industry with their customer-centric brand. Positioning and brand experience go hand in hand. Consistency is so important, and you have to stay the course. And you have to be the guardians of your brand all the time.

Snowflake's board gave us carte blanche to be unique with our brand. At my very first board meeting, Mike Speiser said, "Don't hold back. Make Bob Muglia very, very uncomfortable." With that, we developed more of a consumer-style brand. We wanted to be the market disruptor, but we also wanted to look cool. Our other aim was to become the company everyone wanted to be part of, to work with or work for. So many companies are so afraid and so conservative with their marketing. We were not. At times, our brainstorming sessions in the early days seemed more like a Hollywood movie than Silicon Valley. We had to choose stylish but impactful slogans and designs, quickly, and move on to the next challenge. It worked, because we got it right the first time, most of the time.

Our first bold act did not make financial sense but it made good business sense. It also fired up Snowflake employees. Our founders often talked about the day Snowflake would be big enough to justify a billboard on the US 101 Bayshore freeway that traverses Silicon Valley. We looked at it from the reverse perspective. We're not big yet, so let's look big right now. Everyone was working so hard. Our engineers were architecting and coding around the clock, and sales reps were dialing the phones and pounding the pavement. So, it was kind of a motivational jolt inside the company. But there was another, much more impactful reason to our bottom line.

We started looking for billboard space on the 101. Most marketing teams in small companies with a big budget wouldn't do this. The cost to rent a large billboard along this route was at least $20,000 per month. That was about the average deal size Snowflake's sales team was closing at the time. It was worth it. The billboards—or as we called them, "snowboards"—elevated employee morale, but the main reason for promoting such a tiny company was recruitment. We were ramping up fast and we needed quality people. That section of the 101 moves between San Francisco to the north and San Jose to the south. It's 50 miles of driving past affluent suburbs, where tech, finance, biotech, and professionals from many other leading-edge industries live and work. The 101 connects residents and visitors to two international airports, Stanford University, and eventually UC Berkeley. It was the only marketing channel we thought we couldn't measure.

Our first attempt was a dud. It was on the 101 in Belmont. It was of decent size, but our font was so thin it was nearly unreadable. You had to squint to see it. By then you were already past it. We got it right the second time and secured one of the largest billboards visible to northbound traffic between San Francisco International and the city itself. That was 2016 and we still occupy that space. When we started, our snowboards focused on our product. Snowflake was an unknown. We had to let the world know we existed, what we were selling and how different it was from other data warehouses. We changed the billboard about once a month, so that approach lasted for about half a year. After that, we wanted everyone to know about Snowflake in the context of our values, our brand, and how bold and different a data company could be. Our snowboards then focused on topics such as a new customer, current events, or a notable day of the year. The messages intertwine data topics with something about Snowflake's values. We always tried to be clever, with a twist. Messaging included:

The Data Is In: Love Wins
Celebrating Pride

Feliz Navidata
From the #1 Cloud Data Warehouse

Snowflake | HERSHEY
S'mores Insights In The Data Cloud
Happy Halloween, Bay Area!

To our surprise, everyone knew about that billboard—Uber drivers, tourists, and executives on their way to San Francisco. People posted pictures on social media and journalists wrote about them. We've even received awards. Startups have to stand out, but what you do can't be stupid. It has to reflect your culture and the culture of where you're located. We went on to replicate our snowboards in other major cities in the United States and in other countries. Early on, we had a maximum of what we could pay new hires, and it was lower than what our competitors and other huge tech companies paid people. We offered equity but that wasn't enough. We needed to stand out to get great candidates who were willing to take less money and take a chance on us. Even without the metrics, we knew it was having an impact. We would ask candidates and even employees how they first heard about us. A significant percentage told us it was the billboards.

Our boldness came in other ways, as mentioned in previous chapters. We pushed the boundaries, while trying to avoid stepping over the line and into stupidity. We targeted Teradata, a longtime legacy data warehouse competitor in decline, by offering to migrate their customers to Snowflake. But we didn't target Oracle with such a program, or a billboard near its headquarters on US 101. We were tempted because, like Teradata, Oracle started in the late 1970s. And as Bob once quoted his former Microsoft boss, Bill Gates, "Never get in a fight with someone who's got more money." Oracle had a *lot* more money.

Lastly, make sure to deploy boldness that's in plain sight. Bob was an inspirational leader as Snowflake's first CEO. He led an all-hands meeting every Monday and always painted a picture of what was going to happen next and what we were going to do. He would tell old Microsoft stories to motivate Snowflake employees and provide details of meetings he had with other CEOs and venture capitalists. He is an amazing public speaker—the result of an era when corporations saw the value in employee investment, and trained their executives to deliver keynotes and presentations in front of live audiences almost flawlessly. Bob was a "yes" to live speeches at product launches, and recorded videos and press interviews to promote our significant marketing events. That's where the credibility came from that we desperately needed with customers and the overall market. But many startup CEOs aren't interested in being the face of a company or helping sales close deals. CEOs with that mentality shouldn't be CEOs.

Pillar 5—Alignment with Sales

This pillar is the most important. Marketing efficiency and revenue growth are why this pillar exists. Snowflake's exceptional growth is due to the strong alignment across the entire company—something we've had from the beginning. You succeed only when your marketing programs align 100% with your sales strategy. Otherwise, the majority of your marketing efforts will go to waste, and sales will lose faith in marketing. Alignment starts with sharing the same objectives. At Snowflake, marketing owns the pipeline. Everyone in marketing knows this, so it drives the goals and behavior of the entire team. Sales leaders and their people depend on the quality and quantity of leads. To deliver that, marketing must develop a strategy and execution plan for stuffing a sales pipeline with solid opportunities that will convert to deals. Sometimes I hear people claim that having a certain level of tension between sales and marketing is healthy. I categorically disagree. "Healthy tension" can quickly lead to misunderstandings and create negative attitudes and outcomes. Once that happens, one or both of the teams severs the relationship. At a minimum, alignment and engagement will decline until sales and marketing rarely engage each other. There's a reason for this—history.

The reason Chris and I chose to write this book was the rarity of these two organizations ever being in alignment in most companies. There's too much history to prove this demarcation permeates corporate America. It's how it's always been. That means marketing and sales have to constantly fight this norm. It also means it's too easy to fall back on it and not suffer directly for letting it happen. But the company suffers by way of low efficiency, average sales quota aspirations, disconnected customers, and low company valuation. No amount of product innovation will save a company if the right message isn't getting to the right audiences. Total alignment between marketing and sales overcomes that and drives the rest of your company to do the same. At Snowflake, sales and engineering are in total alignment. It's been that way since day one because it has to be. Engineering and our finance team are in lockstep, as well. They have to be. Our engineers are always planning new features that make our product more efficient. Because we offer consumption-based pricing, better efficiency means lower usage, and our finance team has to factor that into quarterly revenue estimates and budget planning. Marketing and product management are also in alignment. We need to inform them of what's resonating with customers, and product management needs to inform us of what new features are close to production so we can incorporate that into our programs well beyond a press release.

My first duty was to create individual relationships with everyone in sales. When I started, Snowflake had about 30 sales reps, who met on Monday mornings. We had the three territory leaders and eight or nine reps reporting to each of them. Chris and I looked at each one to see who was getting what they needed in terms of leads we were generating and who was not. Are they in the red zone (danger), the orange (caution zone), or were they in the green? I color coded them to measure demand coming in. A rep can get too much demand—more opportunities than they can handle, depending on the territory. And sometimes other reps are sitting there hungry, not getting much of anything. And that's the kind of matching you need to pay attention to, in terms of incoming demand and the capacity to handle it. This approach also covered sales development reps (SDRs), who were junior salespeople and would be a prospect's first contact with Snowflake via email or phone. On Mondays, I would meet with each one of them to review the leads they received and how those opportunities were evolving. Like Chris, I held them to account but for the purposes of constantly improving our marketing efforts. *Have you called on these people? What's working? What's not?*

For me, it was imperative to take that on, so the sales team knew I was engaged and approachable at every level. This is one of many things Chris and I did in the very beginning to create and maintain absolute alignment between sales and marketing.

Establish Your Pillars Early

Each one of our marketing pillars covers, in broad terms, nearly every facet of a marketing organization. They are the foundation upon which you will operate. Yours may be the same or similar to Snowflake's. If you have yet to choose your pillars, are unsure how to choose your pillars, or need to review what you already have, each of our marketing pillars emerged from asking ourselves one simple question.

1. **Positioning**—What is your product and your company all about?
    Too often, startups think they already know what their product is, what potential customers will use it for, and who their target market is. This couldn't be a more myopic approach.

Sure, this is what gives your founders the impetus to start a company but it's not the process to define one. Only from an outside-in approach can you accomplish this. History has shown how the market, competition, and media can shift a company's strategy, product development, and even its name. Be true to your vision but don't ignore the external forces, even when you're still a startup.

2. **Customer-centric**—Where will you focus to deliver absolute success?

    Constantly increasing revenue and profitability is the output of success, not success itself. To achieve both, revenue and profits can't be your first motivation. Yes, making more than you spend is key but you only obtain that result with a much more impactful approach—acquiring and serving customers, and making their success your success. This drives every part of your organization, from engineering to sales, and will drive all of your financial metrics while minimizing the emergence of detractors that sour customer relationships. Such a focus will also determine your relationships with your partners and enable your sales team to compete openly and ethically.

3. **Automation**—How will you accomplish everything, efficiently?

    At Snowflake, we could only take our success so far with the technology we deployed. You don't want to overdo things. Companies, including their marketing organizations, can have dozens or even hundreds of SaaS apps they're paying for each month but aren't really using. At least when software was something shipped to your company, you were reminded of it going to waste as it stared at you from a shelf. SaaS lurks behind the scenes but costs you the same, and could for much longer—out of sight, out of mind. We don't choose software in marketing because it's there. We want to automate a process or develop deeper insight into the customer journey and choose solutions to help us do that.

4. **Boldness**—At what level will you deliver?

    Startups come and go, because most of them fail. Or they limp for a while before failing in one way or another. One of our early engineers once said soon after I arrived at Snowflake, "I've worked at 10 startups! Nine of them failed! I think this one (Snowflake) will make it." Startups fail for one or a number of reasons. Don't allow your marketing organization to contribute to that risk.

5. **Alignment**—Which partner will you serve in order to deliver the most spectacular and measurable results for your company and your stakeholders?

   When marketing doesn't align itself with sales, which happens often, it's aligned with no other organization in a company. Who's left, finance? There's budgetary alignment but that's out of operational necessity. Engineering? That relationship can easily fade as a startup grows. Product management? Unlikely, because product marketing simply takes its cues from product management, which determines a company's product road map. When marketing doesn't align with sales, it aligns with no one. It is an island. Specifically, it's a group of islands that rarely ever interact with one another. Why? Because marketing is allowed to do so, and often does. Being wholly separate from sales bypasses the biggest opportunities for both organizations, and eliminates the one thing that should unite the distinctly different groups that comprise a marketing organization—a reason to strive.

9

Advance Your Sales Team

"Chris, you need to triple, triple, triple, double, double."

—Mike Speiser

A REALLY GOOD startup will achieve a triple, triple, double, double, double in terms of increasing revenue from one year to the next, in its early days. Mike wouldn't settle for that. We charged customers on consumption, so we didn't collect revenue when a deal closed. From there, we had to get each customer up and running on Snowflake and using the product to actually realize revenue.

For fiscal year 2016, we booked $3.5 million in annual recurring revenue (ARR). We more than tripled that for 2017 with $15 million in ARR. We remember someone saying at one of our weekly all-hands meetings: "Holy s–t, how are we going to accomplish that?!" We did. In 2018, we tripled again with $51 million. We did it again for FY2019 with $182 million. That was our triple-triple-triple. Our last full year as a private company, FY2020, we achieved $488 million. FY2021 completed the triple-triple-triple-double-double with $1.2 billion in ARR. We had near-zero attrition for the sales team, which we successfully scaled like no other software company had done in history. Other companies tried and they broke their business. We were moving at light speed, but this thing did not break.

Productivity Model: Amp It up But Soar with Care

Once we received our series D funding in 2017, the board wanted us to go faster on expanding the sales team, faster on targeting new accounts, and faster on closing more deals. They didn't care about the size of the deals. They cared about who the customers were and what problems our engineers were going to solve with new features and functionality. Chad Peets and I continued to work together. Chad had done so much hiring he knew where to look for candidates. EMC's commercial sales division and others like it were a "goldmine," according to Chad, in terms of finding great talent. They hired the right people and taught them how to do pipeline generation. They used John McMahon's MEDDPICC sales qualification, which enterprise sales organizations had adopted widely. Chad and I stuck with the model of making reps productive within six months of hiring them with annual quotas of $1.5 million per rep thereafter. Most tech companies at this stage establish annual quotas of less than $1 million. The key is to double the size of your sales organization and maintain your level of productivity. We continued to measure everything to scale as fast as possible, but avoid putting Snowflake out of business by overcommitting on hiring and underperforming on revenue. I would take our metrics to the board based on the following formula: revenue, minus the yet-to-be-productive reps, and divide by the number of productive reps. On average, if we met or exceeded the $1.5 million revenue number of a sales rep, then the board would have us continue to hire until that number dipped. In addition to that metric, I required reps to have eight sales calls a week and two calls a week with new customers, and to acquire a minimum of two new customers each quarter.

We built the productivity model and then we went to the finance team with our hiring plan. We promoted within and had five to seven reps working for each manager. When you have a new manager, that person can't manage more reps than that because they are developing new reps, interviewing new candidates, understanding the product and helping to close deals. Our sales enablement was very little. I was still the salesperson who knew the most about the product, so I would conduct new-hire training as the reps came on board. They would come to the San Mateo office, and I would whiteboard with them for a couple of days. That was how we onboarded them before marketing had the people and the bandwidth to take this over.

We continued to hire sales engineers and had each engineer supporting two reps. We also created a ratio of how many reps each SDR would support. Again, we measured everything. But this process did have its challenges. Bob and our finance person often disagreed with me on what the quotas should be. At one point, our finance persons wanted me to take on partial quotas for reps who were still in their six-month ramping-up stage. John McMahon told me: "You do that and you're going to get fired." John helped me with all of this, including helping convince Bob that we needed to hire a CMO to establish a demand generation machine that could scale alongside our burgeoning sales organization. If Denise hadn't arrived when she did, I would have continued to run demand gen and then been shown the door.

John put it in military terms to our board: "Think about the sales folks as boots on the ground. But like any army, a salesforce needs air support. And you get that from your marketing people through lead generation." My goal was to get a lot of qualified leads from marketing so the SDRs could follow up on those leads, sales reps could close deals, and the entire sales team would be a lot more productive.

Your decisions matter much more the earlier you're in startup mode. Bigger companies require more time to course-correct, but it also means they can absorb poor choices with less impact. Some may lose their jobs, but it's unlikely the future of the entire company is on the line. Startups are more agile and can change direction more quickly. That also means their window of change closes more quickly. Money is tight: you don't know when your next funding round will happen or for how much. You also risk people leaving on a whim. The departure of key employees in those early days could start a chain reaction among their peers. All you really have is the intelligence, experience, and drive of the people building, positioning, and selling your product. So, give thought to ideas and demands of others who mean well but whose view may only be coming from the context of their domain. As a leader, seek out the advice of those whose mentoring is based on decades of business experience, succeeding and failing in their roles. They will tell you to roll with it, suggest alterations, or go to bat for you to challenge a proposal that would risk your job and your startup's future.

Engineers Scaling Sales

We kept adding features to our product, which helped us close more deals. But like our partners scaling our sales efforts, our engineers had to focus on improvements that would open up new markets at an exponential rate. They enabled Snowflake's data warehouse to support customer compliance with HIPAA (Health Insurance Portability and Accountability Act), allowing us to target the massive healthcare market which must keep patient data secure. Snowflake also obtained certification for SOC 2 (System and Organization Controls 2), which spells out the standards for protecting customer data and is based on five principles—security, availability, processing, integrity, confidentiality and privacy. Any organization that handles customer data requires its software vendors to be SOC 2 compliant. We also enabled our product to be PCI (payment card industry) compliant. Companies that process credit card information have to maintain this compliance, which means so does any product that handles this type of data. These two certifications opened up retail, banking, and other industries for Snowflake.

We continued our engineering efforts to expand geographically, as well. Snowflake was still available on AWS only, and only at its US-west location. For decades, one of the key measures of software has been its performance. The cloud offered near-unlimited data storage and computing power, exponentially more than most companies could provide from their own on-premises data centers. That dramatically improved performance with SaaS products built originally for these computing environments. But the location of those resources was just as important. Latency, the time it takes data to transfer across a network, increases with distance. The closer a customer's data is to their users, the better performance and the lower the latency. This is a metric that SaaS vendors continue to improve—and why AWS and its cloud infrastructure competitors have established data centers around the globe, where SaaS vendors host their solutions. Snowflake deployed on AWS US-east and then expanded to other AWS locations around the globe. These cloud providers also offer locations that meet stricter standards than commercial organizations require, specifically US federal government agencies and the organizations they contract to. Climbing the many rungs of state and federal compliance certifications in order to deploy and sell to these organizations takes years. Think about hiring people who have done this at other SaaS vendors. Otherwise, you will allow your competition to grab market share in government while you sit on the sidelines waiting to enter those markets.

As we mentioned in Chapter 5, we had large customers who would not sign with us unless we offered Snowflake on Microsoft Azure or Google Cloud Platform. They did not want their data stored on AWS because they competed with its parent, Amazon. It's a lot of work for a SaaS vendor to deploy in a different region and a huge endeavor to deploy in another cloud for the first time. These new deployments were inevitable for Snowflake. But timing was everything. Deploying too soon could suck the life out of your engineers. Deciding too late could allow these cloud infrastructure providers to offer what they considered to be their competing data warehouse product. They had dozens and sometimes hundreds of products that a customer could choose from instead of using a possibly better product from a SaaS vendor but one that isn't available on their cloud platform and location of choice. Even if a customer views such products as "good enough," they are already working with a large trusted brand for storage and compute resources. It buys AWS and others the time to improve their products that they position as an alternative to yours in order to gain and retain customers.

Promote Within

Many of our initial salespeople are still at Snowflake. Instead of hiring sales managers from outside, we took our best performers and promoted them. This was counter to how most other technology companies hire sales managers. The view from the industry is to keep your best reps selling. But we had to promote from within in order to triple revenue year after year and double or triple our headcount each year. When our best performers became managers, they didn't have to learn how to sell Snowflake. They only had to learn to lead their reps to sell, and they were able to ramp them up quickly because their boss wasn't just some talking head. Reps would take their managers on sales calls to learn how to sell the product and close deals. The reps had to have knowledge, skills, and a great track record. If they were smart, they were going to pick up the knowledge. If they were driven, they were going to pick up the skills. This was critical because Snowflake is a product that applies to many use cases. Bringing someone in from the outside with a good track record as a sales leader but who doesn't know Snowflake wasn't going to work. In order to lead, you have to know the product better than your sales reps.

From 2016 to 2020, our sales strategy remained relatively the same compared to when I hired Snowflake's first sales reps. Each rep and their managers were responsible for geographic regions. Our sales engineers supported the reps in the sales cycle, but they were also tasked with getting new customers up and running on Snowflake. This was a drain on our sales strategy and made the customer onboarding experience seem disjointed without a team at Snowflake dedicated to this process.

Don't Wait on Professional Services

One thing I screwed up was not establishing a professional services organization sooner. We had a product as a service that was easy to use, and I waited until 2018 to establish a services team. That was a mistake. A services team is essential to making customers and your startup successful. Customers need to get up and running on your product early or they will shelve it. No success there. Our product was, and still is, consumption-based or pay-as-you-go. If they don't use it, Snowflake doesn't stay in business. No success there, either. Our sales engineers needed to support our reps, and nothing else. Moreover, customers don't warm to an ad hoc relationship for training. They want to know in advance what training materials and in-person trainings are available, how soon they can access them, and what other professional services are available once they are up and running on your product. They also need robust product documentation. We produced docs early on, but it was a one-person endeavor that we needed to evolve within a larger services organization.

During these years, we continued to focus on customers already in the cloud or those that made a commitment to cloud computing. As mentioned previously, customers that didn't fit either of these criteria became interested in our data warehouse. This trend increased steadily from 2016, when Snowflake was just 100 employees. Create your professional services team early because product training is just the tip of the iceberg. Key prospects will likely have significant technical requirements as precursors to getting your SaaS product up and running. For Snowflake, we had to help these customers migrate from an on-premises version of our competitor's product to our cloud data warehouse. These endeavors can take months or a year-plus and fall under the domain of your professional services team. Even if you have a partner that does these types of migrations, you must first train them before they are battle ready, and you will likely have to assist them. Partner training to accomplish this has to happen before you sign the customer. Otherwise, a failed or delayed migration could prompt the customer to dump you and let others know about their experience. Either way, they won't be referenceable for a long time, or ever. Before any of this happens, you need to create marketing content to promote such services. Without a services team, I had to lean solely on our content marketing team to produce our first competitive migration guides. There was no one else in the company. They found people at Snowflake with deep technical knowledge of competitors' data warehouses, including one sales engineer who had worked for Teradata. They produced three guides initially and then updated them for a few years before our professional services team took shape and had experts advance these content projects.

Migrations were just some of the technical hurdles customers had to overcome. They also looked to us to make other technical aspirations become realities. They replaced things like secure file transfer protocol (FTP) with Snowflake. Major companies are building their cloud applications on top of Snowflake as the backend data warehouse. And they're using Snowflake's modern data sharing, where data doesn't actually move, as opposed to legacy data transfer methods such as FTP or email. These were just some of the many use cases our customers used Snowflake to replace or complement other technologies, or to take their data strategies to the next level.

Lastly, most customers have data and technology needs that outstrip what a single SaaS product offers. As a product, Snowflake requires other SaaS products to get data into our product and get insights out of that data. But most customers will first attempt to leverage your product for things you may not have considered. Before they do, they will need the help of a professional services team to understand what's possible. From there, other teams within a customer will hear about your product and will inquire about its viability in their parts of the organization. It's easier to expand within an existing customer than to gain a new one. Your professional services team may be their first contact before wanting to speak to a sales rep.

Another Mistake: Delaying Sales Operations

The other thing I screwed up was establishing a sales operations team too late. As you scale a sales organization, you need data-driven ways to define sales territories, log the activity of your sales team, and deploy modern forecasting methods, compensation plans, and systems and processes to quote and book deals. We shortchanged these things because we didn't have the budget. I didn't worry. The bigger you get, the more customers you have, and the more partners you have means your sales deals become more complex. Without the right people and systems in place, all of that stuff can drag down the productivity of the sales team. It's not a glamorous job, but I found that good sales operations professionals make really good money because they're worth it. Sales leaders who find great operations leaders can increase the productivity of the sales team dramatically. Within our first year of operation, we hired our first data scientist so we could advance beyond traditional business intelligence analytics, using AI and ML.

Without such a team, you risk impacting customers, delaying deals, and negatively impacting your sales forecast. You also impact productivity and create friction between sales and other teams in your company. For example, sales ops is the conduit between the salesforce and your IT team. Sales people want the equipment they have to just work. They don't care how or why it might break. They certainly don't want to engage IT directly. When there's no sales ops team, or that team is not aligned with IT, your IT team will battle with you. So, hire fast and hire well. With the hypergrowth a startup can experience, you accumulate technical debt by creating your operations team too late and having to live with the impact of that decision forever.

Once you jump-start your sales operations, there is one fundamental approach you must take regarding your data: Your customer relationship management (CRM) solution is not a data platform. Choosing to store the bulk of your sales data in an actual data platform will revolutionize your sales organization. Data enrichment is a big thing for data operations teams. You want data of all types to serve up to your sales teams and use it to build account scoring or propensity models. The more you know about an account, the more you can pinpoint with data where an account is in your sales funnel.

The traditional method involves buying subscriptions to a number of B2B data providers. From there, you would build connectors to get all of that data into your CRM to enrich each customer record. You would end up with a hoard of data enrichment tools all running their automations inside of your CRM. You also overwhelm your sales people with more data than they can digest and issues of data accuracy. To combat this problem, we had the B2B data providers deliver data via our modern data sharing method. We got that data into our data platform and did all of our enrichment in an automated fashion within the platform. We end up with this beautiful master account data and then we push only what we need back into our CRM. We built an account propensity score (APS)—the likelihood that a customer will buy. We developed a method to measure lifetime value: If they buy, how much will they spend? Then, we just push those data points back to our CRM, rather than all of the data from the data providers. From there, reps can run a report to see all of the accounts in their territory by APS score to determine which ones they should focus on at any point in time.

Managing our data this way also gave us advantages in terms of how nimble we were and our ability to scale with a smaller sales operations team. When you size an operations team, you often think about the number of quota-carrying salespeople compared to how many operations people you need. Not long after we launched sales operations, we had a 13-to-1 ratio. That's pretty lean. In most companies under $2 billion in revenue, you're looking at a 5-to-1 ratio. So, we had less than half the team that a lot of companies would have. A lot of it has to do with how well we leverage data. There's still a lot more we can do with automation to expand sales operations to support more reps in a non-linear way.

Choosing a CRO: Hire or Promote?

Mike Speiser mentioned in the foreword of this book that I rose to every challenge in the early days of Snowflake, eventually earning the title and responsibility of CRO. But that was never the plan. I was a district sales manager at EMC when I joined Snowflake. From that day forward, the board believed they would hire someone with more experience, and I would report to them. Bob Muglia remembered receiving a call from Mike in 2018. He wanted to discuss having me head North America sales and hire a global head of sales over me. I was coming up to five years at Snowflake. Bob asked Mike: "What has Chris not done? He's never missed a number, he's one of the best recruiters I've ever met, and he's a very good manager." Bob added that Snowflake didn't need a president or chief customer officer. What we really needed was a CRO—someone to drive the sales part of the business.

Bob and Mike discussed some of the requirements for that role, but what the board really cared about was whether or not I could hire senior leaders such as a senior vice president of sales for North America. John McMahon put it this way: If you can't hire someone better than yourself underneath you, then we'll hire someone better than you and above you. At the time, the board was focused on hiring above or below me for North America. I had never operated at the scale of a CRO or a senior vice president. Either way, a much more experienced salesperson had to join Snowflake. I did hire someone underneath me who understood how to build a sales organization better than I knew how. Without that person, I would have likely failed in either role.

That was the test that the board was waiting to see me pass. The board never said they wanted to get rid of me. They wanted me to operate at a higher level, so they tested me and they pushed me, which I think is the way people can become great. When the board named me CRO, the title made it a lot easier for me to recruit talent. All of a sudden it became clear I was at Snowflake for the long haul. That also meant I had to embrace the whole concept of scale yourself. I loved helping close big deals in the early days of Snowflake. As CRO, I had to resign as a deal jockey, because that would no longer be my job. As you ascend in any organization, you have to direct your team, and

10

Absolute Alignment Between Marketing and Sales

"You can't compete with each other if you want to compete with the rest of the world."

—Chris Degnan & Denise Persson

THE NUMBER ONE problem we see in enterprise technology companies is the friction between sales and marketing. There is a lot of finger-pointing when things aren't going well, and it starts at the top. Both of us serve on a number of company boards and tell them what we do when we discover a problem. We identify it and agree on it, together. There's no finger-pointing. Of course, we've had our challenges but we fix them, one way or another, because we had a great working relationship. It's incredibly important that the relationship remains positive. Every single sales leader told us, "I can't believe how good our marketing department is." In a lot of companies, you don't often hear that.

It's vital for leaders and managers to figure out who you can trust. Sales can't do everything they need to be successful. Marketing has to own demand generation and the sales pipeline. On the flip side, marketing's success will be constrained if they're not serving the sales team. Snowflake offers an enterprise solution. Marketing's job is to help drive every transaction between a salesperson and a customer.

We have to ask ourselves, "How can we make that process easier?" Marketing is primarily about creating customer awareness, increasing demand, moving prospects down the sales funnel, and helping close customer deals. We strive to educate prospects about how our product can solve their problems. We reach out to our customers to gain their feedback and help us promote Snowflake. But it all starts with the relationship, the alignment, between sales and marketing. If there isn't a good relationship, that's our fault. We're the ones to blame. We don't blame each other. If one of us hired the wrong person, we can't blame that person. We need to determine why we hired that person and what went wrong.

Build Trust Early

Do something that will make this happen because alignment is built on trust. Neither will evolve on their own, and there's a huge gap between not having a reason to trust someone and actually trusting them. The sales team at Snowflake had to run its own demand generation function before marketing arrived. That team was made up of both young and experienced professionals who picked up the phone or sent emails to identify prospects and set meetings with them. When the marketing team arrived, it took over demand generation. We both knew how key it was to the success of the sales organization. As the number of quality leads continued to pour in, we came to trust each other implicitly. There has been a huge positive correlation between the success of sales and the strength of the relationship between our two organizations.

Smaller deals can close within 50–60 days once they enter our pipeline. Large enterprise opportunities can take months or even years. In the early days of Snowflake, it was hard because we were an unknown quantity. The marketing team focused a lot of their energy on getting customers to sign up for a free trial of our product. Initially, salespeople were not allowed to forecast deals unless the customer had trialed our product. It was about getting the product into customers' hands and showing them how it could fix their problems and create new opportunities. Marketing focused nearly all of its attention on that while we started building brand awareness.

Both teams saw the hamster-driven process to sign up for a free trial as the first of many opportunities for marketing to earn the trust of sales. The product experience of the trial was sound. But getting prospects up and running with the product was another story. We suspected that once we fully automated the trial sign-up process it would ignite a storm of growth. The activation of a free trial was probably our strongest signal that an account was ready to engage sales. It included $400 worth of free consumption of data storage and computing. The offer attracted a lot of prospects but resulted in very few trial activations. It was our first experience of "killing the hamsters" in sales and marketing.

Early on, a lot of things were done manually. So, we established a strategic initiative in 2017 to automate everything we could in order to increase our productivity. For the trial, prospects signed up via our website, but that's where the automation began and ended. They received a message right then and there, stating that we would notify them in the next day or so about their trial activation. From there, a service ticket was opened by a human, who had to review the information supplied by the prospect, verify their identity, confirm they were not from a country known for hacking software companies, manually activate the trial, and then notify each prospect via email that their trial was ready. For a technology company, it was not a ringing endorsement of Snowflake. It was absolutely not set up to scale, considering that our website was generating a level of interest that screamed for automation. It took a significant amount of resources to automate the activation in a relatively short period of time, but we got it done.

It didn't end there. The activations happened in real time but only a portion of signups still resulted in prospects trialing our product. They needed more help from us. Marketing needed to own everything around the trial, but we also needed to own every step before the trial. So, we created a virtual office hour that taught prospects on how to get started with Snowflake and how to create a proof of concept within the dollar limit of the trial. So, we had to set ourselves up to scale in a way where we did not overwhelm the sales reps. They understood the product the best but had limited bandwidth to be inundated with prospects who weren't ready. And we needed to do that in a big, one-to-many way.

So, we made it marketing's responsibility to increase traffic to the website, enable a scalable process for product demos, and have each prospect speak with a live customer in a very transparent way. With everything we did, our goal was to take prospects through that journey. At that point, the prospect was ready to have a conversation with sales and vice versa. Once they did, we considered them a qualified lead. It gave us a green light to continue to hire new reps at a superfast rate. If we couldn't do that, we were dead. We wouldn't be able to make our targets. On the other hand, if we achieved that or better, then the response from the board would be, "Let's pour gasoline on this. Let's scale it up." Funding for more headcount rested on automating and scaling free trials. Today, trials result in 30–40 percent of our lead flow.

Establishing Alignment

There are two types of CMOs. Those who come from a product marketing background and those who built their careers in demand generation. Ultimately, what salespeople want from the marketing team are leads. Snowflake's marketing team does a bunch of other stuff. They handle product marketing, field marketing, public relations, content marketing, and many other responsibilities. Everyone on those teams echoes marketing's mantra: sales is my number one customer, and we're a customer-led company. Some marketing leaders might not see it that way, and they're making a big mistake. It's someone who has an ego and thinks marketing is more important than sales. "I'm the straw that stirs the drink and I'm gonna tell sales what to do." It could also be a marketer who is unable to execute on their strategy. Or, it's a sales manager who has rarely relied on marketing and isn't about to start. Keep these people out of your organizations. From the top down, marketing must be empathetic with how sales operates, and sales must know their success depends on their relationship with marketing. It's all about how marketing can make sales reps' jobs more efficient and their lives much easier.

From day one, we tell marketers, "You can make mistakes but you can't piss off our sales organization. If a sales person comes to you for something, you can't say 'no.' You have to listen and understand what they're asking for. You have to be service-oriented and solutions-oriented to serve sales." Salespeople aren't prone to waste marketers' time. If they were, they'd be wasting their own time, which they don't have much of to spare. Once a salesperson knows they're in lockstep with marketing, they're going to reach out for help. When they do, it's because they need something done they can't do themselves or don't have the bandwidth to, and they want to scale their efforts by deploying marketing. Once this happens, and every marketer delivers to their counterparts in sales, then trust emerges and it's there to stay.

Cascading Your Alignment

It has to come from the top. In the early days, we met three times a week and we worked to make that happen down to the next level, and the next. Sales makes its quarterly business review meetings available to all of marketing. Many startups say they are engineering-led companies or product-led companies. We are a customer-led company, and that's what unites us. In 2016, marketing took over demand gen and built trust with sales by delivering on its promise to make it a success. This was huge, because marketing owning demand gen was not the industry norm. Everyone crossed their fingers. Alongside automating free trials, it was the first major act of establishing trust between sales and marketing. It worked and everyone was a witness.

We first aligned sales and marketing around our "What Matters," which we discussed in Chapter 7. Now that we're a big company, we have shared OKRs (objectives and key results) that align across the company, keeping us focused on our priorities. Everyone in marketing knew, at every level, how they aligned with their counterparts in sales—vice presidents, senior directors, managers, and individual contributors. Nothing would slip through, no one had a hall pass, and no bad behavior was allowed. The successful sales people look at themselves as leaders. When you're selling data platform technology such as Snowflake, you can't be the lone wolf. You have to mobilize all of the sales and marketing resources you can get.

Others saw that success and the impact spread. People talked about it until the entire sales organization was imbued with the notion and expectation that marketing was an enabler of their success. Most of our sales reps came from previous companies where this wasn't the case.

"I've worked with marketing teams that had no clue," one rep said. "They focused on things that didn't matter to me," another said. They were shocked when they arrived at Snowflake, and their reaction accelerated the validation of our approach to marketing.

When misalignment was present, it was often people-related. It was the wrong person in sales or marketing, and we took those people out of the organization. They were me-me leaders. More importantly, we would let each other know about anyone on the other person's team that was not aligned. Neither of us became defensive. We would look into it and make a decision, either way. We relentlessly defended the culture, which was a culture of extreme alignment and still is today. We always had the mantra of "no rep left behind."

Marketing Driving Sales Efficiency

Sales efficiency is not about having 30 percent of your reps blowing out their number. It's about having at least 90 percent of your reps meeting their number. When your efficiency reaches that level of your productivity, you continue to hire. We had metrics for the reps—such as how many qualified meetings they were getting each quarter from our demand gen efforts. We didn't look at whether or not a sales district was successful. We looked at sales success at the rep level. It's about the efficient use of resources to get necessary results. It's misguided to have salespeople prospecting on their own. Having them working on junior level tasks, such as following up on potential sales leads, is inefficient. Salespeople are very expensive, even when they're on commission. If they don't make their commission or their bonus, they will leave and go somewhere else. Then you lose a year of investment in them. The best use of their time is having conversations with qualified prospects and advancing those opportunities. At the same time, you must have a cadence of demand generation to avoid the trickle—tsunami of generating leads for your SDRs. You needed to know when to step on the gas and when to step on the brakes in order to keep a fast but manageable pace.

This whole process is about building and scaling, building and scaling. As each person ascends in sales or marketing, they need to step back from a few responsibilities and pass them on to the people who work for them. It's a never-ending evolution. Without it, you'll remain stuck. It's all about the people you surround yourself with. Organizations that thrive only hire under the people you've developed because they've succeeded in taking the next step. If you have to hire over them, then it's time for them to move on from your company. If we hadn't done so at Snowflake, we wouldn't be here. You also have to keep out egos and politics, because it's counter to your culture. It's like a sports team. When there's too much competition within the team, they start losing. Sadly, that still happens in most organizations. There's so much mistrust and misalignment in organizations, and it holds them back. It creates dysfunction. You don't trust each other's intentions or you don't trust their competence. You can be smart but you first have to have trust. And you only gain trust when you deliver. Marketing delivering for sales and sales delivering for customers.

Executing on Alignment with Sales

Every team in a startup's marketing organization has a reason to align with their sales organization. But the level of alignment with sales is not uniform across each marketing team. Some teams have infrequent exposure to sales but that does not mean they are misaligned. It means they rely on other teams in marketing to convey sales strategies and feedback required to create and tweak their marketing strategies and programs. These teams that provide such conduits often work more closely with sales. Others have daily communications with sales and meet weekly with their counterparts. They are tasked with delivering the highest impact to sales and are detailed below.

Demand Generation

A lot of demand gen is simply a function of your budget. As mentioned in Chapter 7, we spent a lot of money. We scheduled the week in such a way that we had different nurturing points that generated new demand every day, moving existing prospects further down the sales funnel. We didn't want to just throw a lead to sales randomly because someone had perused our website or downloaded a white paper. They had to take a number of actions with us. What we do in marketing is identify the prospects we should go after. Then we address the issues we know are important to them and educate them about what we can do for their organization. When the time is right, they say, "Okay, now we're ready to look at Snowflake." That's when we hand them over to sales.

In addition to our outbound campaigns via email, social media, and other mass-marketing channels, one of our big projects was redesigning the website. Every one of our campaigns had to point prospects to our website. In 2016, the website was mostly information-only—not atypical for a startup with around 100 people. We chose Lars and his demand gen team to own the website. It served us well. We assume anyone who visits our website doesn't know much about Snowflake. When prospects come to the site, there's multiple, clear paths for tech and business professionals to explore the product and our company. All of the elements of a website—branding, messaging, content—were the best we could deliver but the website was almost entirely a demand generation vehicle.

The questions were, how do we drive exponentially more people to the website, and do we have a site that can handle that level of traffic? By stress testing the website, it became clear it wasn't an effective destination. We needed to redesign it. We needed to make a better mousetrap essentially in order to capture inbound traffic. We went to work, designing a new home page and a few different templates for the technology pages. We designed all of them to maximize prospects' time on the site, provide value-based information and insights, and get them to fill out a form to download a piece of content, register for one of our many events, or request that we contact them directly. Normally, 3 percent of website traffic converts into a lead. After we redesigned ours, conversion shot up to 10 percent. It costs a lot of money to do that, but driving traffic is expensive and absolutely necessary. You can't go out and claim that you are the new leader in a category if people type in "data warehousing" and other companies' websites are listed above ours.

Five years later, we moved ownership of the website from demand generation to our corporate marketing team. Demand gen was still the focus, but the site became useful for many groups at Snowflake and is now shared by all of them. HR uses it as a vehicle to communicate with employees, list job postings, and attract new talent. Investor relations uses it as a place for analysts and investors to see our latest earnings results and see how the business is doing. Professional services uses it to communicate with customers. Training uses it to onboard new employees. We host product documentation, and the community team uses it to stay engaged with our incredible developer and user communities.

Franchises and Sonic Booms We're constantly identifying new prospects and nurturing them toward contact with a sales rep. Alongside that, we established what we call franchise programs—something that is repeatable, scalable, and attracts hundreds or thousands of prospects on a weekly basis. Our live product demos, self-service product trials, and virtual and instructor-led labs to get up and running on Snowflake are some of our franchises. We had money to spend, but we also had to be budget-conscious in those early days. These scalable franchises, which seem expensive, can be extremely economical when comparing inputs to outputs.

Our sonic booms came soon after marketing arrived. They are our biggest programs and events that deliver the most impact. They serve many purposes, such as establishing market presence and brand awareness, generating demand, and making a startup appear much bigger than it is. Early on, we created Data for Breakfast. It was our first event series and something we've been doing since 2018. It happens in a morning and includes about five impactful sessions led by Snowflake product folks, partners, and customers. It started in just a few major US cities and expanded to more than 100 locations around the world. We know exactly how our partners integrate with these types of events. We know exactly what audiences we're targeting, and what the cost will be. And we scaled it without having to hire a commensurate number of additional employees. We produced creative branding that we tweak slightly every year and made it easy to change focus from one season to the next based on what topics were most important to technology and business professionals. Having these key franchises that we can duplicate each year allows us to scale insanely fast and deliver campaigns on a budget.

Our annual user conference, Summit, is an all-hands-on-deck event. The inaugural Summit happened in 2019. Planning starts just a few weeks after the previous year's event—just enough time for every Snowflake to catch their breath. Timing the very first one was key. Start too early in your startup phase and you've portrayed to your customers how small your business really is. Wait too long and customers start clamoring about when you will announce your product's newest features and functionality. They may even start questioning the viability of your company. Snowflake's Summit is the utter and complete manifestation of alignment across marketing, between marketing and sales, and across the company functionally and globally. Product marketing drives Summit and enlists and orchestrates every other marketing team to make the event a massive success. Our Events team handles planning and logistics. But at its heart, Summit is where we announce to the world what new technologies will be available with our product. The whole event starts with product marketing working with product management, to convey Snowflake's release of our newest features and functionality. From there, the genesis of each Summit emerges. Our sales and alliances teams are in lockstep, driving thousands of customers and partners from around the world to attend the event. Our first summit attracted a few thousand people, increasing fivefold in just five years.

Also in 2019, we started what is now our Snowflake World Tour—that happens globally to get our message in front of potential customers, and educate them with a one-day version of Summit. It's a compressed version of our annual conference and focuses more on prospects versus existing customers. As eager as a prospect might be to attend Summit, that's a multi-day physical event that could be hard to justify the expense to a manager or finance team if you're not already a customer. Over time, we realized that 12 months between annual conferences was quite a gap from a marketing perspective. In response, we created our annual Build conference, which targets Snowflake's developer community, where we similarly make new product announcements and offer a host of product hands-on events for data professionals.

These and many other franchises and sonic booms happen year round at Snowflake. They work together like an orchestra—many sections coming together but each roaring up or easing back at different times so as not to overwhelm the audience at any one time.

Even though marketing drives these programs, sales is in lockstep. We only schedule a live event in a city if we have a sales presence there, that person or team is ready and able to attend, they have their own prospects attending, the reps eventually respond to the leads the event generates, and marketing nurtures to a point when sale engagement makes sense.

We're also measuring constantly and getting insights back in real time. That allows us to move at a much greater speed, which is a competitive differentiator when activating campaigns. You can grow fast only if you are able to move fast, or change direction, in real time. Data allowed us to iterate on the fly, adapting our marketing channels to focus on what was working and what wasn't. We're always promoting something, a webinar or an ebook or a live event, and using multiple channels to do that. If a channel isn't working, then we eliminate it and put our resources somewhere else in the market. You don't need to waste time or money on a channel that isn't performing for us. Remain open to feedback from your sales organization. Never take offense to someone telling you a campaign or event didn't attract enough of the right people. If the value isn't there, try something different.

Partner Marketing

Working with partners brings different benefits at different stages of a startup. Partnering with organizations much bigger than your own, by size or reputation, brings with it credibility to your customers. Other partners that have a specific focus can help your startup enter industries or accounts sooner and easier than you could on your own. These are sales strategies that worked for Snowflake in our early days and can work for you. All of these reasons justify engaging partners to execute joint marketing programs as well. But there's one more crucial reason to market with partners—scale, reach, and cost.

We achieved three times the reach at one-third the cost. We typically partnered with one or two partners on marketing campaigns, content, and events. We paid equal portions and shared the leads with all partners involved. But you can't choose marketing partners if they're not aligned with your sales organization. Sure, we partner with the big companies, AWS and Microsoft, and with growth companies that are our size or slightly larger and still growing rapidly. But you have to be geographically aligned with their sales organizations. Our partner marketing organization maintains the marketing relationship with partners. You can deliver programs but there's no reason to do so if the partner doesn't have a sales presence in the area you're targeting, for example. Market together and then show up alone to meet the customer? We did make exceptions. One of our ETL partners was new and didn't have any substantial field sales infrastructure in place. Yet that partner's product made it much easier to load data into Snowflake, which was critical before people could start using our data warehouse. They helped get data into Snowflake and we helped them get into accounts. We were once in their shoes, and a more market-entrenched partner extended us the same exception because our technology brought additional value to the sales opportunities they brought us into.

Account-Based Marketing

Of all the areas in marketing to align with sales, account-based marketing (ABM) is the absolute perfect fit between the two organizations. It is a version of demand generation but delivers marketing programs directed at specific companies strategic to your sales strategy. We were early with ABM and known for doing it very well. We went all in, built the infrastructure from scratch and aligned with sales on the individual accounts they cared about. This spread like wildfire across our sales organization because they had never seen anything like it. When we hired new reps, it became a recruiting tool. "Here are your named accounts and marketing is going to create engagement for you." We built a machine and nobody wanted to miss out.

Our ABM strategy emerged around 2017, when Snowflake created a named account sales team and populated it with senior field sales reps. They identified key organizations that had massive deal-sized potential. Our ABM team developed a plan to generate awareness within these accounts with concentrated messaging across specific channels and targeted at influencers inside the prospects' key lines of business. We implemented fully bespoke campaigns to more than one thousand prospect accounts. They included custom messaging and micro websites, and other forms of marketing that delivered our value proposition based on the account's pain points, topics of interest, and challenges common to their vertical industries. Often with ABM, the individuals you're trying to reach are unknown to you at first. Or if they are known to you, their current level of intent is not. We deployed a number of tools that identified and measured the intent of an account in near-real time. These tools identify the topics that accounts were actively researching and how often. This intent data can also indicate if the account is so engaged with certain topics specific to your technology that it may be on a path to purchase a solution. Your ABM strategy can also scale to a one-to-few strategy, where you deliver the same value proposition to multiple named accounts in the same industry. To execute your strategy, assemble cross-functional teams consisting of members from ABM, field marketing, partner marketing, sales development, and field sales reps.

Ride the Pipeline Together

Our sales and marketing teams align for weekly sales calls, with all levels of stakeholders to discuss pipeline and forecasts. Our sales managers and reps discuss the deals they're progressing and how they're actioning the marketing leads they've received. Marketers on the call talk about how inbound leads are evolving into meetings thanks to our SDRs, to opportunities qualified by our account executives and how those deals are progressing. That call happens every week throughout our sales organization with marketers, including field marketing, ABM and demand gen who talk with sales about how they're supporting the sales business. That's why the sales analytics team, which includes the people who create the dashboards to enable that call, use our marketing data so they can distill it throughout the rest of the organization. If your sales and marketing teams aren't talking, you can't build the right metrics, you won't have access to the right data, and you can't think about how to structure that in a way to make a productive call with all of the teams involved.

Marketing owns the scoring model that looks at people who register for or attend our marketing events. Once they're there, we can sort them by their different persona types and understand what's the profile of people who are attending those events. Of those leads, we understand who has the highest propensity to take a meeting with Snowflake and to open a new opportunity. Certainly, we have an executive focus, but we also send the SDR or the sales rep a notification to follow up with those people we've deemed high priority, whether they are a prospect or existing customer. That model learns from past events, by learning about the attributes of a prospect's journey with Snowflake that led to a successful outcome. So, we want to make sure those people are prioritized for sales to follow up with. From there, we determine which ones are converting into meetings and which ones are converting into opportunities. This enables the marketing teams to inspect their campaigns and understand how successful they were at driving sales outcomes.

Be Straight with Each Other

Alignment doesn't work if neither team can tell the other that something or someone is not working out. Sales and marketing teams that aren't aligned resort to bad behavior when these issues arise. By the time it becomes infectious, your company has suffered in a number of ways that affect its viability, or at least stall its upward trajectory. Sales and marketing teams that are perfectly aligned always have the success of your startup, your customers, and that of their counterparts as their top priority. When issues must be addressed, no matter how sensitive, anyone at any level should feel comfortable raising it with their counterpart in sales or marketing immediately, and with their manager, if need be. This will further strengthen the alignment between your sales and marketing organizations.

11

From Product to Platform

"Customers have a line item in their budget for a data warehouse."
—Chris Degnan

EARLY IN THIS book we stated that our founding engineers realized they were building a data platform that could handle different types of data workloads, including cloud data warehousing. As a startup, Snowflake leadership made a strategic decision to position Snowflake as a data warehouse built for the cloud. Any prospect intent on analyzing their data had a data warehouse and had the budget to maintain their existing product and possibly upgrade to something new. Our exercise to determine our market position confirmed that Snowflake should be a cloud data warehouse. This decision served our customers and Snowflake well for about three years.

Two significant market forces caused us to rebrand Snowflake to what it really was—a cloud data platform, which is a solution that has many uses. The first market force is common with all products that are technologically diverse. Customers use your product based on how you position it. But their lens is not product-based, it's problem- and opportunity-based. They buy solutions to solve data problems and create new business opportunities that never stop emerging. It makes sense they will leverage their existing solutions in ways beyond their malleable boundaries set by SaaS vendors' product positioning.

During our first few years, customers applied our product to workloads other than data warehousing. The product was already able to handle these workloads, so our customers went for it.

The second market force was the competition, young and old. Snowflake was disrupting the data warehouse market. Our customers lauded Snowflake for our technological achievements and the impact we had on their business. We were way ahead of our competitors and we were getting noticed. Their initial response was to adopt our messaging as their own. They also made negative claims about our technology. Then there were partners of ours that became competitors once they claimed their data solutions could also handle data warehousing workloads. Without joining in their mudslinging, we had to reciprocate by positioning Snowflake as a product that could capably handle data warehousing and other data workloads that were the bread and butter of our competitors. We also had to acknowledge the industry reality that any competitor worth their salt would develop similar functionality to ours in the next two to three years. Knowing that, our product management and engineering teams have to plan for and develop new features respectively that would continue to serve our customers and keep us ahead of the pack. With all this known, it made sense to position our product to reveal what it was already capable of.

To accomplish this, we underwent another, yet stripped down, version of our initial positioning exercise to confirm Snowflake should be marketed as a cloud data platform. Our technology was not yet the go-to choice for these other data workloads, but we had enough features and functionality to expand from one workload, data warehousing, to five workloads—data lake, data science, data engineering, data sharing, and data warehousing. It was a significant, cross-functional marketing endeavor that required a new strategy, messaging, content, sales support tools, and more, including relaunching the product and the company.

Stay True to Sales

We accomplished this in just a few months. It was an enormous transition even for a growing startup that was still very nimble. Yet, sales remained in two minds, understandably. They welcomed the additional opportunities a platform could offer. They also had customers wondering how they should proceed with their cloud data warehouse vendor. The notion of a platform required sales reps to explain in detail that we were still the same company. Sales reps also had forecasted deals focused for data warehousing workloads, requiring the same conversations from our prospects. If we had created four new products, this wouldn't have been an issue for sales. But Snowflake has only ever sold one product, with new workloads being added every so often based on how customers continue to use our product and how we continue to evolve our product. By doing so, customers and prospects need assurance that your product will continue to meet their needs. It's common for prospects to have a data warehouse or a data lake as a budget line item. A broader data platform of any kind doesn't get such specificity. So, it's up to marketing and sales to tell prospects how a platform will help them solve their data problems across a number of use cases. But sales needs marketing's help.

Product Marketing to the Rescue

Crafting new messaging once you reposition to a platform is key. Consider how it will accurately rebrand your product and your startup. More nuanced, give consideration as to how it will help or possibly hinder your sales organization. Reason being, executive management determines a startups topline messaging, with inputs from maybe one or two marketing vice presidents. Sales has less influence in this process, so be sure to advocate for their input.

Conversely, startups are all but bootstrapped to going all in with messaging about what their product is and what it isn't. The need to assuage customers and prospects is challenged by the market, analysts, media, and the competition referring to your product what it was, not what you say it has justifiably become. The only true latitude you have to help your sales reps explain to prospects and customers what your platform offers is through sales enablement.

At Snowflake, product marketing is responsible for developing sales enablement tools—training materials, sales pitch decks, competitive guides, and host of other content that educates your sales team and helps them educate prospects. Ensure your product marketing team remains open-minded with sales when reworking all of your sales enablement tools to coincide with a repositioning of your product.

This is the one area in which sales has complete say as to how these resources will transform, and how they won't, so they can continue to sell with little to no disruption. A SaaS company can transform itself in a matter of days, weeks, or months, depending on the size of the task. Customers and prospects need much longer to get comfortable with that transition. And don't worry about over-rotating or not going far enough when changing sales enablement tools. Only some of that content sees the light of day when presented to customers. You can gain feedback from sales and tweak it as needed.

The key is continuity. Sales enablement content can't contradict your startup's topline messaging. Otherwise, your sales reps will experience very awkward sales calls when a prospect points to your slide deck, and then to the homepage of your website, and says: "Please explain." There is still plenty of latitude for adjusting customer-facing sales enablement content in the shadow of an extreme shift in company messaging. It's a balancing act that product marketing and sales need to accomplish through iteration and feel solid when done. Otherwise, your reps will end up in customer meetings, walking a tightrope.

PHASE III
Scale

12

Hiring, Retention, and Parting Ways

"We made plenty of hiring mistakes early on."
—Denise Persson & Chris Degnan

...NOT BECAUSE THEY were bad people. It was simply the wrong place at the wrong time for them. It's not their fault or yours. Most people eventually land in the right place.

Values are so important when you're scaling a startup. If you mishire from a culture standpoint, you impact the entire team. Our values have been our North Star in terms of how we behave. There are examples of people who didn't last on the sales side. They were phenomenal in terms of sales but just didn't work with our culture. Our culture was the antidote. It kind of pushed these people out. When you have a strong culture, it becomes obvious when someone doesn't fit. Of course, you can't see all of that when you're interviewing someone. For marketing, you must have empathy and understand the craft of sales, and really work as a team with sales. That's the most important thing.

There's also the ability to execute really well. You need a scrappy mindset. You have to know you have scarce resources. When you work for large organizations, it becomes very easy to just sit in meetings, brainstorm things, and push slide decks across departments.

Your Network, and Theirs

We've mentioned this previously. In the early days of your startup, hiring people who you have worked with before is key. You know almost everything about them—their work ethic, what they value, how they treat others, their ability to evolve, and more. From there, you can trust that your first hires will choose those who have worked for or with them previously. When you build an organization as a sales or marketing leader, your personal reputation is super important. You need to have a following of people who want to work for you again and again. This transcends to everyone you hire. You will hire college grads with abundant energy and willingness to learn and succeed, while remaining honest and humble. Their closest friends will be of the same pedigree.

There is one exception to this steadfast rule. One of the early hires in marketing had an impressive work history that spanned multiple continents. This person had only returned to the United States recently after working for many years abroad. As a result, he had no following in Silicon Valley. He had interviewed with one of us at a company previous to Snowflake. He was offered that job but chose to work for a more traditional software company. That was the only experience we had of him before asking him to come and interview at Snowflake. He worked out well as an individual contributor. When it came time to scale his responsibilities, he hired a competent professional who knew many people with amazing talents. He realized this weakness of his and alleviated it by hiring for talent and resources. He deployed many of them as contractors to further scale his operations during those early years. His strategy also helped ensure his team's success as the budget would not warrant another permanent position on his team for another year.

Those Who Can Scale Themselves

Startups require many things from early employees. You and the people you hire in the early years of your startup need to operate at different levels. At the very beginning, we were very hands-on. Soon, there were other people doing that for us. Everyone has to elevate at the pace of the business. You can't be in the weeds in every area as you ascend. Leadership becomes more important in terms of building an organization with the right composition of people, while providing clarity, setting expectations, and more, as you scale. You have to love change. You have to realize that the requirements of yesterday will not be the same tomorrow. And you have to be curious and foresee what's going to be needed when moving forward.

That begs the question: If individual contributors learn from their managers, who do managers and senior executives learn from? We spend time with other sales and marketing execs who lead bigger organizations and learn from them. We read and listen to other influential people whose experience and wisdom will benefit us as leaders. We all need to adapt and change to whatever our roles demand from us now and down the road. There have been so many at Snowflake who rose to that challenge, embracing the opportunity of reinventing themselves. As a leader, you have to innovate both with time and with what the organization needs. You have to be very curious and learn from others. And part of that is mastering the art of cross-functional alignment. It's a different level of alignment—horizontally and vertically within sales and marketing, and between any two or more teams within your startup. You also need to gradually introduce new people into the organization who have experience at different stages of a company. No one has all the experience necessary to operate from the zero-dollar stage to the $10 billion stage. It's incredibly important to introduce the right people into your organization at the right stage. All the while, we have to evolve ourselves, and we have to evolve our organizations.

Passionate But Not Provocative

When you become bigger, you must have a certain level of patience for things. People who shoot from the hip and are very emotional often don't work at the speed a successful startup requires. When you work with more people, you have to be level-headed. Don't think in extremes, because what you think is going to impact 10,000 other employees. It's not just about maneuvering or being diplomatic. It's about the art of getting things done with many people. Not everyone can do that. You have to think about the consequences of your actions. Otherwise, you're going to slow things down. You have to think in advance about your decisions downstream and cross-functionally, and how those decisions are going to impact people. Strategy and planning are super important. You must also have a mentality of trust within the rest of the organization. Don't say "those people in finance." If you take that approach, you're dead. It's "our friends" in finance. We're one team. Those who can't handle that don't work out for long.

Choose Aptitude Over Skill

As a leader, you have to be good at spotting talent and potential. You'll make mistakes, but you must force yourself to learn. If you have to choose, hire for aptitude over experience. If a candidate has both, that's ideal. People with aptitude are going to find a way to succeed and serve your business and your customers in the process. Those who have succeeded at Snowflake find a way no matter what. Hiring managers have to determine who has the will to succeed. How hungry is this person, really? So many people are not. Are they willing to learn? Are they willing to put in the work? Will they work well with others? Do they fit in with our values? Do they have integrity? Most importantly, can you say "yes" about them to all of these questions?

As a leader, you must hire those who know more than you. This is nothing new, yet the problem persists. In marketing especially, there are so many distinctly different functions that a head of marketing can't possibly master them all. But they should know enough to spot the right talent. The same goes for sales. It's not just a mass of account managers; there are also professional services, sales operations, and a host of other teams that don't carry a quota but report to a startup's sales leader. Hire people who have the attributes we discuss in this chapter. They also need to be experts in their domain—so much so that senior leadership may, but shouldn't, feel intimidated by the aptitude and skills of a frontline manager or a senior individual contributor.

Smart But Humble

We discussed in Chapter 3 about how important it is to hire smart salespeople. The same goes for marketing. Software technology requires someone with the intelligence to understand your product well enough to market and sell it. They may not have earned a college or master's degree in computer science or mathematics, but they should be curious and smart enough to understand how it works and what business benefits it can deliver. Often in startups, it's your engineers who are the masters of explaining your technology in ways that salespeople and marketers can understand. From there, these business professionals must have such a working knowledge of your product that they can ask a string of questions to understand it even better. If they don't, then they won't know what they're talking or writing about, and so too won't your prospects and customers.

No matter how smart they are, everyone must balance their intelligence, aptitude, and accomplishments with the humility and gratitude your coworkers deserve. Without those two finer qualities exhibited across your startup, a toxic work environment ensues, your customers suffer, and you jeopardize the future of your business. Not because your strategy or technology are substandard, but because your egos crowded your judgment.

Executive Referrals

Say "no" to the wrong candidate even if executive management or your board recommended them. Snowflake hired a number of leaders early on that were shown the door after a year or less. Board members and executives gave them glowing recommendations. Nearly all of them had the skills for the job at that time, but they didn't fit our culture. Some could execute but couldn't develop a strategy later on. Others were great at strategy but couldn't execute thereafter, or just weren't able to operate at the speed of a startup. Worse off, the more senior the role, the longer it takes to determine if someone is going to be successful. You have to afford them at least 9 to 12 months to show results from the bigger initiatives they're entrusted to deliver. Only when they fail can you justify reevaluating their future.

It's quite the quandary having to reject a high-level candidate solidly referred by someone above you, or taking a chance on them only to face the agonizing experience of letting them go a year later. Best to make it clear to the board and executive management that their referrals will receive no more consideration than unknowns who have the necessary skills to occupy the role. For both types of candidates, a shiny resume and even good interviewing skills aren't enough to determine if a candidate is right for your business. Hiring the right person at the right time is a combination of their innate attributes, as discussed in this chapter, and taking a chance. When you fail at this, you have to fail fast. When you know it's not going to work out, be swift with that decision. Then, question yourself as to what you could have done differently. When you hire the wrong person, there's no mystery about why you had to let them go. Work out why so you don't repeat. Otherwise, you tarnish your reputation and risk losing the right employees. Because it takes longer to assess whether or not a manager will succeed, they've likely disgruntled the people who report to them along the way. One or two of these managers will make the right people lose faith and leave.

Capitalize on Strengths to Retain Your Employees

As a marketing leader, you need to know what your responsibility is, what's required of you, and what you expect from the people who work for you. At times, the leaders themselves don't know what they're supposed to do because marketing has so many different roles. When I grew up in the 1980s and the 1990s, the focus was on your weaknesses and how you addressed them. Today, it's about leveraging your strengths, your personal superpower, day in and day out. We're never going to be good at something that we're not meant to be good at. On the other hand, if I have a team of 300 people firing every single day on their superpowers, we can accomplish three times as much and create more happiness in the process.

Over the years, and as our marketing team grew, we undertook a process to understand our strengths via a psychometric tool in the form of a simple questionnaire. From there, each person in marketing receives an accurate and lengthy description of the type of professional they are and in which job attributes they excel. Each of us is placed on a spectrum based on each of our individual strengths. It's quite a revealing process to each individual and for all of us as a team. Once we receive our individual results, we meet as a team to understand each other's strengths, so we know how to best approach each other on a daily basis to leverage those strengths.

Field marketers, for example, tend to be rah-rah types, championing our sales team and our customers. But others are well suited for analyzing data and evaluating our marketing campaigns. We need those people as well to understand, in real time, what is working and what is not. Then there are those who value making decisions. We need them too. There are others still who like to build systems and love the processes that enable those systems. Yet, we would never have them work with the salespeople or our customers. Not because they can't. It's just not their strength but it is the strength of others on our marketing team. They're best suited to be in a marketing role that doesn't require that kind of outgoing, extroverted personality.

After the test, we even moved people around. They were effective in one role but not wholly inspired and therefore not firing on all cylinders. For example, we moved one person from a role that had him engaging solely with his Snowflake colleagues. The assessment revealed he had the woo thing—the ability to build and maintain positive relationships with many different people even if they were difficult to approach initially or known to be resistant. He loved building those relationships. So, we moved him to a role that focused on working with partners of Snowflake—partners from our business ecosystem that were key to our success. He thrived. So did others we moved based on the results of the assessment. One aspect of our jobs is to hire the right people at the right time and in the right roles. Soon after, we ensure they are in the right roles, or not, and adjust accordingly.

This has always been an incredible tool in determining who was in the right marketing role when we first arrived at Snowflake. It continues to provide impact in helping us create more accurate job descriptions and confirming that we chose the best candidate for a role. Lastly, this process is an incredible team-building experience. Sure, an offsite or a social event can help people to get to know each other outside of their jobs. But getting to know people in relation to their jobs, and how to productively engage them and capitalize on their strengths, is an incredible advantage for an organization. This has to happen early on for a startup to be successful. Unfortunately, most startups don't take advantage of this opportunity.

Working at Speed

Throughout this book, we have discussed the work ethic at Snowflake, and we've often characterized it as "working at speed." Our offices are delightful places, filled with professionals who embrace our values and meet most or all of the criteria we recommend startups use to screen candidates. Working at speed refers to the efficiency required in the workplace to advance your operation. Using the right mix of in-person meetings, video calls, email, and instant messaging apps to develop strategies and deliver on those strategies is one example. The questions we often ask ourselves are: *Is such a meeting necessary, and what will we achieve? Am I inviting only the essential people? Why should I attend that meeting? Is my presence essential to the meeting's success?*

When we discuss a strategy or program, we encourage input and get straight to the matter. When we make decisions, we start executing from that moment forward—not next week, next month, or next quarter. We support each other and hold each other to account. If someone is vague on what they have set out to achieve, we help them clarify their goals. We do so because we measure everything.

We greet each other every morning when we arrive at a Snowflake office. Then we get to work, holding ourselves accountable to our company values in everything we do. We have lunch together in our cafeterias, and we still host the weekly and monthly social events that first emerged when the number of Snowflake employees could be counted on two hands. We exhale throughout the day by meandering to any of our well-appointed kitchens, saying hello to anyone who we run into, and having brief chats before we get back to work.

Working at speed means being efficient, so things happen at speed. In the very early days of your startup, your founders and first engineers will likely work long hours. Getting to market quickly with a sound product is their goal. They also know this phase will taper off as you hire more engineers and your product becomes generally available. Having an unspoken but company-wide culture of long hours with no end in sight will cause higher than normal attrition and develop a reputation that will cause solid candidates to consider startups other than yours as their next career move. While working, in the office or at home, operating at speed is what preserves employees' health and sanity, and allows them the time to enjoy their lives outside of work. Keep that in mind. You can have amazing results, outpace your competition, and lead your industry. Just avoid mowing down your employees to get there.

Saying So Long

When your startup has dozens or even a few hundred employees, how departing employees leave your business is important. We had near-zero attrition during the early years at Snowflake. When people did leave, we made their exit as positive as possible for them and their coworkers. We took one employee to lunch, and hosted a drinks event for the entire company to say goodbye to another person who had joined Snowflake early on. We acknowledged our appreciation of departing employees, which helped boost team morale.

We've talked about hiring people who see change in a company as an opportunity to grow and succeed. Some don't, and that's not always easy to determine during job interviews. They may deliver big impact for a period of time. Then it becomes clear they aren't able to evolve with your business. Everyone at a growing company is susceptible to this situation. Identify it, work with that person, and then determine if they can move with the times, or not.

13

Build for a Billion

"Frank was right. I had to reorganize the sales so we could go to the next phase of growth."

—Chris Degnan

BOB MUGLIA COINED the phrase "build for a billion" at Snowflake. It would become our annual gross revenue target for the fiscal year 2021, and a goal that would set us in motion to attain that number and beyond. Bob once said that to take a company from $100 million to $1 billion, you have to hire salespeople and engineers like crazy. He also said the hardest part of growing a company that fast is managing the surge in new employees and keeping everyone aligned. The requirements of leadership continue to change as you grow. Eventually, as a CEO, you are managing leaders who are experts in their areas. They have control over their part of the business. So, your job is really just to help them work together effectively, and make sure the right things are happening. Leadership is really about three things: strategy, structure, and people.

Yet, Bob wouldn't be CEO when Snowflake reached a billion dollars. In April 2019, the Snowflake board announced that Frank Slootman would replace him. Bob was a product guy and an amazing leader. He has tons of executive credibility and can easily engage a customer's chief technology officer (CTO) to help close a deal.

He spent five years at Snowflake getting us in front of technical leaders during the sales process, among other things. He was well known and the reason we were able to close a number of large deals with big customers before we crawled out from under the viability apprehension customers associate with all startups. Yet, Snowflake was advancing quickly into a new phase that required skills and experiences not every CEO has. Successful startups move through these phases quickly, requiring a change in leadership sooner than larger organizations demand. This is universal. Frank as CEO when Bob was at the helm wouldn't have made any more sense than Bob being CEO during Frank's tenure.

Frank was born in the Netherlands and moved to the United States not long after he finished his undergraduate and graduate degrees from Erasmus University Rotterdam. In 2003, he rose to his first CEO role at Data Domain. He led the company to its IPO in 2007. EMC acquired Data Domain in 2009 and Frank left in 2011. Frank joined Service-Now that same year as its CEO. He expanded the company's total addressable market significantly by repositioning its product from just a help-desk solution to an enterprise software solution. A year later, he led ServiceNow to its IPO and then departed in 2017, taking two years off before joining Snowflake.

Restructure Your Sales Team for Growth

During its first five years, we built a very high transactional commercial sales organization. We focused on signing new customers with smaller deals. We had an inside sales team that engaged customers via phone and email, focusing on companies that had up to 250 employees. Our field sales team handled everything else. The two teams were organized by geographical territories, without any segmentation based on a customer's industry, annual revenue, or if they were part of the Fortune 500 or any other recognized list of companies.

Frank came in and said, "You've accidentally gotten business at large, well-known companies. But you're treating them the same way you're treating the commercial accounts that are spending $200k a year with you. You can't do that." Then he said: "You're going to rip the Band-Aid off." People like to wait until the end of the fiscal year to effect any changes to a sales organization. Our sales reps were already four months down the road with their existing quotas and compensation packages. With Frank now at the helm, we had to reorganize our entire North America sales organization now, not later.

We reorganized our existing structure into three new sales teams:

- **Inside sales** – A high-velocity team of reps closing about 12 new digital-native customers a year that were startups and could sign a deal with us after a one- or two-month sales cycle. Many of these customers would end up spending $1 million a year or more on Snowflake. We still have this sales motion today, landing a customer in their infancy and growing the account. We could get these reps productive (selling to their quota) in about three to six months.
- **Enterprise** – Field reps who were productive after about six to nine months, focusing on mid-market sized customers. These were field sales professionals who had sold enterprise software at other tech firms and had already been through the motions of learning a new technology and a new sales process.
- **Majors** – Field reps who covered our top 250 global accounts, which could spend $10 million or more a year on Snowflake. These reps had deep experience working large accounts and required 9 to 18 months to be productive, because large accounts move at a much slower sales pace.

Frank was right. I had to reorganize the sales team so that we could go to the next phase of growth. It was hard, making decisions quickly and acting on those decisions. Reorganizing the sales organization accomplished a few things. We had reps with the right experience serving the right customers. The motion to acquire a new customer is much harder and very different from expanding the opportunity within an existing customer. Even though they're small, digital-native, and only in the cloud, acquiring such a new customer means they are betting on your product to help run most or all of their data operations. Managing a single multinational, in one way, is similar to managing 20 or 30 commercial accounts. But those business units are crossing into different subsidiaries, product categories, and countries.

The Frank Factor and Business Value

Frank was helpful with our "land and expand" sales motion. In the early days, we didn't compete with the legacy vendors—Teradata, Oracle, IBM Netezza, and HP Vertica. If we went into an enterprise of any size and said to them, "We're going to replace your legacy system," they would have laughed us out of the room. Instead, we were hyper-focused on landing a single use case or data workload. Frank is a larger-than-life tech CEO, and you could use his name to get in front of chief executives and boards of directors of Fortune 500 companies. They would take meetings with him to discuss the business value they could obtain by using our technology. All of a sudden, we were in this top-down sales motion with a seat at the table with CEOs.

That's when the magic started to happen for us. That's when we started getting these monster opportunities. We were getting big deals before, but this was the evolution of the $100 million deals with Frank. Customers went from looking at us as some promising startup to a real company. Bob was really good at getting in front of the heads of product and CTOs. He could go toe to toe with them. Frank didn't want to have those conversations. He wanted to talk to CEOs about what they wanted to hear—how Snowflake could create new market opportunities, increase revenue and profit margins, and even pivot a company from its traditional product offering to a data and software applications provider. We got a ton of value from both Bob and Frank.

Soon after the reorg, we added a vertical sales element to the majors team. Because we were getting into these CEO-level meetings, we had to help the customer understand what business value they would gain from our product. This is why you have to build industry-specific verticals. We created teams for financial services, media, entertainment, telco, and tech. We also had persona-based selling within each of these industries, selling to the CEO, CFO, and down the line. So, we went from just a majors sales team to majors with an industry element. That sales team has to still support the largest 250 accounts or so. These are the things you need to consider when expanding and focusing a sales organization. This go-to-market strategy also included industry-specific solutions and messaging on the marketing side, and an ecosystem of partners to help deliver business value for each vertical. We gave these customers a complete solutions approach.

Make Your CEO Sell

Frank and Bob were involved in critical sales deals during their tenures as CEO. Not every startup CEO has their clout. That shouldn't matter. Whether your CEO creates sales opportunities or helps close them, that person should have the willingness to join an opportunity at the request of your sales leaders. There are many who won't. They feel their technical brilliance is enough of a contribution and they deserve to stay within the walls of your startup. Others of the same background don't have the confidence to engage customers. Some have too much confidence because your startup may not be their first rodeo. Others still have had a very successful career climbing the ladder at a large company, or have already reaped the benefits of leading a previous startup that was wildly successful and went public. Frank once said, "Chris, money messes you up. It makes you think you're better than you actually are." My kids think I'm still the same dude. I don't want to change their view of me or that of my customers or colleagues.

CEO involvement in sales isn't just about helping to close deals. It's about understanding your potential customers and their problems, getting invaluable insights from them about their industries, and further building your CEO's credibility. They should go on sales calls. Customers drive your product road map. If a startup CEO sits at their ivory table, they will make decisions not based in reality. You can see that in some founding CEOs. They think the company is successful because of them. Success comes from the skills, experience, and dedication of every employee, not just the CEO. There are plenty of salespeople who have left Snowflake, thinking they could recreate the success they had at Snowflake but couldn't. I've been at some really hopeless companies. They weren't failures because of me but they certainly weren't successful because of just me, either. I joined the right company at the right time and applied everything I knew, and learned everything I could to help Snowflake succeed. It doesn't make me any more important.

Case in point: Frank arrived at Snowflake just about a year before the spread of Covid was declared a pandemic. We vacated our office space and relied on phone and video conferencing to conduct business over the next year. Snowflake was a vibrant place to work, with the exchange of ideas and information in face-to-face meetings, from one adjacent desktop to the next, while stopping by one of our kitchens for a snack, and at our weekly and monthly social gatherings at our campuses. That all came to an end. Yet, Frank kept the fire burning with his Monday morning emails to the entire company. In them, he discussed meetings he had with customer CEOs via video. Frank is also a voracious reader and loves reading history. He weaved together what customers communicated to him, the insights he gained as a three-time startup CEO and the wisdom he gleaned from books to inspire us for the week ahead. Frank helped reconnect what Covid severed. Those emails resonated with the entire company. But without those customer sentiments, we all would have lost what we call our "North Star" at Snowflake. He continued his weekly emails once we returned to the office.

During all phases of your startup, your CEO has to be involved in sales, whether your head of sales requires your CEO's help or your CEO has the clout to get a meeting with a CEO at a top customer. Even the most talented, professional, and respected head of sales has boundaries, boundaries that are set by the customer. Tech sales people have come a long way in recent decades. They have to be partners to their customers and long after they sign a deal. As altruism in sales reps has evolved, they're still responsible for a quota and customers never forget that. They won't judge you by that motive alone but they will need something else, or someone else, who will assure them that your company will be around for the long haul. Your CEO and the rest of your executive leadership team should be able to explain the future of your product and your startup, and how you will help enable and enhance the future of a customer's business.

Bring Sales Recruitment in House

When I started as the first Snowflake salesperson, I didn't trust anyone to generate demand or leads for me, so I kept that function for myself. Then I realized I couldn't continue to manage it and needed someone else who could do it better. Denise took it over almost immediately because she had the same sense of urgency. Demand gen became an ever-evolving machine, working in lockstep with sales as we continued to transform the sales organization for hypergrowth. Marketing ended up delivering more than 90 percent of our qualified leads.

When Frank arrived, it came time to transfer the SDR function to Denise because she has the same sense of urgency. It also made sense, organizationally. The SDRs are those people who have first exposure to prospects. They are the ones who follow up with new prospects after those prospects respond to one of our many lead generation campaigns. They are the first sales people to touch a lead.

Chad Peets and I had worked well together, recruiting hundreds of sales reps as we exceeded the annual quotas given to us from Snowflake's board, and later our finance team. When Frank arrived, along with our new CFO Mike Scarpelli, they began preparing to take Snowflake public. It became time to move sales recruitment in-house. We didn't have to hire for a startup profile anymore, and we needed to take on every part of recruitment ourselves. Chad worked with Frank for about nine months to train Snowflake people how to recruit new sales reps. It's normal to contract out major functions within a department before you develop a critical mass of people. Eventually, you have to move those functions inside your operations or you'll never be able to leverage and transcend that experience and value that would otherwise rest with an outside service vendor.

Transfer Sales Development to Marketing

The team of SDRs is the main juncture between sales and marketing. It is where marketing develops programs and the SDRs generate leads based on those programs. SDRs are measured on how they qualify leads to a point where they set up a meeting between a prospect and a sales account executive. Each SDR is mapped to two account executives at Snowflake. That's how sales development aligns with the rest of sales.

Under which organization should the SDRs be—sales or marketing? Our industry peers on both sides ask us this question often. There's more than one answer. Early on, it made sense to have SDRs under sales. They are building the sales pipeline but they are also a sales talent pipeline. The vast majority of them have aspirations to be account executives. Yet, we moved that team under marketing in 2020 because sales operates as individuals, with each one responsible for accounts based on a geographic territory, industry, or size of the customer. Understandably, they see any support they get from anywhere in your company to serve their customers and achieve their quota. What can arise is account executives steering SDRs in a number of directions that makes sense for the account executives as individuals. That can work for customers but creates the risk of SDRs becoming glorified administrative assistants, making it hard to measure your SDR investment.

We moved sales development to marketing for programmatic purposes. When you have a few dozen SDRs, having them report into sales makes sense. When you have a few hundred SDRs, you have to look at scaling their impact programmatically. Everything needs to be the same—onboarding, training, and making them successful at breaking into new accounts and expanding your presence within existing accounts. What's crucial to this transition is that your sales and marketing organizations are already perfectly aligned. So, when sales development shifts from sales to marketing, nothing drops out from that transition. You're evolving SDR success, not sacrificing aspects of their success. All three entities involved—sales, marketing, and the transitioned team—gain from such strategic decisions.

There was also the data. We reviewed the SDRs' prospecting activity: Where were they spending their time, who were they reaching out to, and what accounts were they focusing on? We also ran a report on which accounts were most engaged with our demand gen efforts. We asked where the inbound leads came from, who was showing up at our events, and who was downloading our content. There was about 20 percent overlap in those two spheres of activity, which meant the SDRs and demand gen were not always targeting the same accounts. This had to be fixed. Marketing is a machine that has unique tools at its disposal that are purpose-built for driving awareness, engagement, and opportunity. The SDRs are the secret ingredient to making all of those things successful. When you put a human on the end of those inbound lead journeys, and you embed a human in those outbound ABM programs, it's such an accelerant. We can see how much faster those programs, coupled with SDR engagement, move opportunities down the sales funnel. On the flip side, an SDR could target accounts on their own and reach out to them without any marketing support. But when an SDR was paired with an ABM program, they generated three times more meetings within those accounts versus with just outbound cold calling.

A CEO'S Product Pivot

When everyone is heads down, it can be hard to see what's next for your product. The ink was barely dry on our cloud data platform messaging when Frank arrived. The companies he had run or worked for were not in the same tech market space as Snowflake, so there was some initial concern about the impact he could have early on. That also meant he had fresh eyes on how we should position the product. The new workloads we added to our go-to-market strategy were the inspiration behind pivoting from "the data warehouse built for the cloud" to "the cloud data platform." But Frank saw much more for the product beyond the data platform. During media interviews and when speaking at events, he started talking about the "data cloud." He distinguished it as a revolutionary alternative to where data is traditionally stored—instead of in each application an organization uses or with a cloud infrastructure provider. He hammered on, accurately claiming that both of those options siloed customers' data, making it near impossible to unify, share, and analyze all of that data scattered across an organization. He took it further, revealing the business impact of companies without such access to their data. They would be less competitive, unable to truly serve their customers, and would be left behind when it came to constantly innovating. By having a storage layer between cloud infrastructure and all of the applications that run a business, organizations would unlock the most value from their data.

His view was gaining traction with the market, so we got to work to make Snowflake synonymous with the data cloud. It wasn't a direct shift from the cloud data platform to the data cloud. Our first was to message Snowflake as a product that had two elements—the data cloud and the cloud data platform. The former was mostly about the storage and access to data. The cloud data platform was about the use cases or data workloads you could implement with the product. This approach lasted months, not years, and had to be sunsetted for clarity and go-to-market purposes. It was a challenge to market the product this way, which meant it would be much harder for customers to distinguish what Snowflake offered via our top-line messaging. We made it too hard and eventually went all in on the data cloud, breaking that down into logical domains of what the product offered. We didn't lose "platform," the data cloud just absorbed that aspect. It worked.

Your CEO runs your company. They should have experience with operations, which is a critical element to your startup's success. They also have to lead, establishing your culture and making sure everyone is living your company values, among other responsibilities. They also have to be a visionary, looking toward the future and steering a business that will wholly represent what your product is capable of. Sadly, there are too many software companies that have mediocre products but overzealous marketing and high-pressure sales strategies. These companies make money, go public, and either limp for years or are acquired. On the flip side, to underrepresent what your product is truly capable of produces just the opposite effect. Customers see your offering as a point solution, not something that can drive their entire business forward. Tragic, because their problems are bigger than your product, so they're always attempting to use software in ways it was never intended. Yet, it shouldn't always be on them to figure that out and then tell you about it. They need their tech vendors to position, sell, and deploy their solutions in ways that accurately reveal what those solutions can accomplish. In the end, don't over- or under-position your product.

Make the Abstract Concrete

Many tech startups want the market to view their solution as a platform, so they position it as such. Whether or not they truly offer a platform, they have a bigger task when marketing and selling their solution as such. A platform is abstract from the very beginning, so a startup has to quickly define what makes theirs a platform. Most don't. If they try hard but can't, then they most likely have a point solution, such as an app or a tool. In that case, they help automate a specific part of a business or enable software developers to create apps or manage data throughout its life cycle. A platform can do both, and much more, depending on the platform.

At Snowflake, we defined it quickly, clearly, and concisely at the top of our website and everywhere else our platform messaging appeared. We convey what the product does, how it differs from the competition, and what business value customers could experience by deploying Snowflake. Many tech firms don't accomplish this. Their messaging resembles more a vision or mission statement, with a focus on the company and not the product. Or, they make very broad benefit statements. The prompts target personas to ask the question: "What does their product actually do and why should I care?" When we pivoted to the data cloud, we created even more distance between the abstract and the concrete. But our data cloud messaging included the benefits of where and how the data was stored. From there, we explained what you could do with the data and what you could build on top of the platform piece of the data cloud. In essence, we took the same approach previously when pivoting from the data warehouse built for the cloud to the cloud data platform. We just spent more time to succinctly clarify what the data cloud is.

A new CEO or other c-level executive will bring new perspectives as to what's possible with your product or expand your product positioning to articulate everything your product can do. Listen to them. From a single use case to a platform, and beyond, a technology company will see these upstrokes early if their product can deliver on such new promises. Always look around the next corner. Otherwise, you will steer your product and your company by staring at its wake.

Amping Up

Working hard and working smart are not opposite work ethics. They've been positioned that way for decades and wrongly so. Working smart will cause you to work harder but less time doing so. Startups are notoriously associated with 16-hour work days and seven-day work weeks. When your organization reaches about a hundred employees, those multi-hat work horses evolve into small teams with shared responsibilities. That doesn't mean people become any less productive. Snowflake eclipsed the hundred employee mark about three years after its founding. Engineering was the biggest team, then sales, marketing, and a few people handling operations. All of the teams moved with intensity. We worked manageable days and maybe a few hours on weekends. When we work, we're efficient, make decisions quickly, and take action on those decisions the same day. Startups have the ability to be that nimble and can easily change direction once a decision reveals itself to be the wrong one. Without intent and intensity, nimbleness and creativity remain untapped.

When Frank arrived, he got us to a whole other level. While he was CEO, he wrote a book, *Amp It Up*. In it, he focuses on a number of strategies and tactics to deliver greater impact at a faster pace. "My basic advice was to keep playing your game but amp things up dramatically. Raise your standards, pick up the pace, sharpen your focus, and align your people. You don't need to bring in reams of consultants to examine everything that is going on. What you need on day one is to ratchet up expectations, energy, urgency and intensity."[1] In his Monday morning emails to the company and during quarterly all-hands meetings, Frank set the table for amping up Snowflake, company-wide. He would drop a nugget of advice, more like a mandate, as to how Snowflake employees and managers should increase the pace and impact of their endeavors. He would detail what it meant to "go direct"—find the person that has the answer or can address a problem and contact them directly. If they are outside your organization, don't pass it off to others in your organization—up, down or lateral—with the hope they will do the inquiring for you. Instead, cut across departmental lines and reach out to that person to mitigate the number of humans involved and maintain a fast pace.

Frank also stipulated that we "manage down, not up" at Snowflake. If you're stuck, seek advice from your manager but don't pass off the issue to them. Managers are there to help you solve problems, not solve them for you. Think about how you could solve it, discuss it with your manager, and move forward. Managers are also in place to inspire, empower, and delegate to their teams. If someone is always going to their manager, team performance suffers and so does the ability for that team to operate and serve other teams within and across other departments.

Operating in overdrive should be your goal. Think airplane instead of a car. A car engine operates at a fraction of its total available horsepower. Every so often we put the pedal to the metal when we're nearing a deadline or when an issue emerges that needs immediate action. The rest of the time your organization is cruising along at normal velocity with the gas pedal barely down from its

---

[1] Frank Slootman, *Amp It Up: Leading for Hypergrowth by Raising Expectations, Increasing Urgency, and Elevating Intensity*.

free-resting position. A plane engine is designed to operate at 100 percent capacity and sustain that output for long periods of time. A plane also picks the straightest path to its destination and gets there much sooner, and at a much higher speed. So, don't bemoan a startup founder or CEO who wants to amp things up for good reason. Venture funding isn't inevitable or endless. Existing competitors won't stand by idle while you disrupt them. The next bright founder and competitor won't hesitate to get started and beat you to delivering a commercially available product. But again, be wary of a leader who drives employees to work crazy hours, thinking that will deliver impact. Working smart requires executive insight, strategy, and execution so employees lead happy and healthy work lives, with time left to be with family and friends, while enjoying their downtime.

14

Bottom-Up Sales

"Our SDRs are involved at all levels of sales."

—Denise Persson

PRESENTING TO CUSTOMERS, progressing deals, negotiating contracts, and closing business are things that can never stop. That's what experienced account executives (AEs) are really good at. The other thing that can never stop is the idea of prospecting—the constant outreach and marketing follow-up with potential customers to grow the business of the company. That's why sales development exists and why it is one of the most impactful sales motions a startup needs in order to survive, thrive, and evolve into a global powerhouse.

Your SDRs' mission is to identify and advance new opportunities within new and existing customers so your account execs can move those opportunities down the sales funnel and convert them into deals. This happens within two domains at Snowflake. The first is having an always-on execution for responding to inbound demand. When people respond to an offer, visit our website, download our content, or sign up for an event, and they have a relevant title at a company we care about, our SDRs engage them further, educate them, and qualify them. You can't afford to let that play out organically and hope that prospect keeps heading down that journey on their own. The SDR team is there to shepherd them into their next engagement with your company and potentially into a conversation with an account exec. The second motion of SDRs is to execute highly targeted and highly sophisticated outbound motions to accomplish the same goal. Someone filling out a form is just one aspect of high-quality demand. Today's buyers will search online, engage with advertising, talk to a colleague, or educate themselves with resources outside of your company's website. SDRs, supported by ABM and with the direction of field sales, use these additional signals to tailor their outbound campaigns toward targeted accounts. These two motions are the day-to-day function of sales development, SDRs are measured on setting meetings with qualified prospects to grow the sales pipeline and fuel the growth of the company. We've made quite a few innovations on how that works versus the traditional concept of outbound sales that most companies think about.

More Than a Rite of Passage

SDRs are not just a sales pipeline. They're also a talent pipeline and the future of your sales organization. Most companies don't think about or invest in this idea. They think of SDRs as junior, high-activity, churn and burn, low-skilled resources who are cold calling lists all day long. Snowflake sees this program as the entrée into great tech careers for young, promising talent. We also recruit talented individuals coming from outside the tech industry and those who are further along in their careers. Sales development is the meritocratic breeding ground of internal talent and internal leadership at your company. That's an explicit goal we have articulated at Snowflake. The best output of that strategy is Chris Degnan. He was our first SDR, sales rep, and a bunch of other things all rolled into one. The board told him from the very beginning they would eventually hire a sales exec above him. Chris evolved to become Snowflake's CRO, and did so with the guidance available to him in those early days. He also worked his tail off. Snowflake SDRs have so much more available to them in order to succeed. More than half of Snowflake's account execs started as SDRs, and we expect that proportion to increase. At our annual sales kickoff events, gracing the stage are account execs who started as SDRs and who win awards for closing some of the most important deals with our most prominent customers. But an SDR's progression isn't limited to sales. They have become successful pre-sales engineers and marketers, and have joined teams other than sales and marketing at Snowflake.

All of these stories are the result of a strategy that most companies gloss over and instead execute a plan to work SDRs hard for 12 months. If they flame out, they're replaceable. Those who survive will get a shot at the next step, but it's all on them to make that happen. That's a very different philosophy than developing a career path for SDRs to become quota-carrying account execs. The key contrast is the investment and development you put into SDRs to enable that journey and to support them along that journey.

Choosing and Developing Your SDRs

The hiring profile for SDRs is important. College grads just out of school with some internship or professional experience can be good candidates. Others include those who switch careers and become successful SDRs, and later on, account execs. They've been working for a while in another industry and realize only then what they really want to do. We hired someone who worked for more than a decade, developing a successful career in financial services but didn't see that future for himself. He became an SDR, and he grew to become a senior leader in the SDR ranks. We also hire folks who are former educators and teachers coming into the role. They are a really good fit. We get veterans who enter the private sector after their military service. It's high potential, hard-working, high-aptitude people from a number of different backgrounds who make good SDR candidates. Yet, it's a shell shock coming into B2B software for the first time and learning about a very sophisticated platform such as Snowflake and the data space in which we play. It's all very new, and there's a very steep learning curve to the art and process of sales. The SDR role offers everything candidates need to know to become successful.

Most companies have some semblance of sales onboarding. They train their account execs, while SDRs shadow them for a short time before they hit the ground running. Hopefully, they soak up some information and then go figure out the rest. For SDRs to be successful, they need dedicated onboarding and enablement with a curriculum built just for them. So, it's meeting them where they're at when they come through the door of your company. It's not focused on discounting prices, developing sales quotes, and completing order forms—all that and other stuff that salespeople care about. It's centered on product training and the sales pitch, competitive differentiation, how to position your product, and learning about the space and your customer personas. The key difference here is that some companies have onboarding for SDRs or salespeople, but very few companies have a structured development path of continuously building the skills of SDRs, along their entire journey. Snowflake SDRs will hear from our sales engineers about how to pitch our technology or talk about generative AI. They'll hear from those really seasoned, former SDRs who are now crushing it as account execs in the company about what it takes to get to the next level of sales. Then we'll put them through pitch simulations and client discovery call simulations, we'll certify them for those skills, and we'll continue to develop their knowledge formally and continuously throughout their time as SDRs.

It's also about teaching them how to use the virtual cockpit that displays all of the technology that we equip salespeople with. At Snowflake, there's an orchestrated tech stack at play that SDRs train on and navigate. Then, it's teaching them about the working relationships inside of the company that are critical to their success. For example, they learn everything about the account execs they'll be working closely with and how to develop a territory strategy with that person. All of this comes from a sales development enablement team that puts together a curriculum and manages SDR onboarding. We put them through rigorous onboarding, training, and certification. Most companies don't have dedicated training for their SDRs but likely do for their account execs. Sad, because SDRs are often the most junior of all teams in the sales organization and need the most training to become successful. Ultimately, we formalize their readiness for the next step in their career—interview readiness and skills readiness so they can apply for an account exec role and be completely confident doing so.

All of this training should be centralized, easily accessible, and also used as a recruiting tool. The Snowflake Sales Development Academy has its own branded microsite. The academy attracts so many applicants that only 3 percent gain admission. That's lower than many top universities. It details the opportunity and benefits of joining

Snowflake as an SDR, and explains the first month of onboarding and the following 14 months of sales certification and promotion readiness. The site also introduces potential candidates to SDRs, who tell their story about their time in the job and what opportunities they've ascended to in Snowflake's sales team. The microsite also links to our corporate website, where candidates can learn more about Snowflake's culture, the company, and our technology.

When we onboard SDRs, we set the tone for how they're going to work inside Snowflake and explain clearly what their job entails. The most important relationship they have at Snowflake, even more than with their frontline SDR manager, is the relationship they have with their account execs. We have formal education and curriculum for the SDRs on how to build trust and build a working relationship with those account execs. We map each SDR to two account execs, exclusively. They find and advance sales opportunities before passing them on to their account execs. It's a mentoring relationship. We want the SDRs to learn from the account execs, to be taught by them and receive feedback from them.

We prescribe a hip-to-hip, SDR-account exec relationship—two business partners working a territory together via weekly meetings, daily conversations, and reviewing all of the signals an SDR monitors to identify and engage top-of-funnel opportunities they will develop and eventually pass on to an account exec. For example: "I know that XYZ financial institution is going to develop a large language model (LLM) app for its end consumers to do better banking." The SDR then helps determine the right marketing narrative based on their account research, and works with ABM to position Snowflake to help address that problem. The tangible handoff is an SDR qualifying the opportunity to a level of certainty that they produce a meeting between the prospect and the account exec. That is the formal handoff. From there, it's up to the account exec to further qualify the prospect as a real deal forecasted in the pipeline.

Identifying Prospects Based on Intent

Accounts that salespeople and SDRs co-target will have whitespaces for an SDR to fill. What line of business should we target? What Snowflake value prop will resonate? What contacts do we have or not yet have in our CRM? SaaS products built to measure intent are one type of solution we use in our marketing tech stack to fill that white space. They give us a hypothesis around a particular company and what technology topics their employees might care about at any given moment. Still, we may not know the names or titles of these people. We only know who they work for because intent is measured by the search activity of people who connect to the Internet via the IP address of companies that SDRs want to target with specific campaigns. We then look at who is landing on our website and is there a spike in website traffic from those IP addresses. We incorporate other conversion points that we have ongoing with our weekly events, such as our office hours, hands-on labs, and the customer experience with our product and with our trial. Their activity on technology topics reveals to SDRs the types of programs we then run with the help of Snowflake's ABM team. For example, that intent informs the display ads and the offers they contain that we're going to surface to people with that same IP address. Ultimately, the conversion points that we're going to put in front of these people, such as landing pages and content, will hopefully get them to opt in and reveal themselves. That's one vector that surfaces interest and de-anonymizes people who we should be paying attention to in the companies we want to target.

Yet, as your product offering expands, or your existing customers have found more use cases to apply your product, you have to listen to more attributes. That's a blessing and a curse. Snowflake has evolved from a cloud data warehouse to a cloud data platform to the AI Data Cloud. It necessitates broadening what you're listening for and expands the surface area of what you need to train people to understand internally. Your account execs and SDRs need to understand more products and more use cases. Then there's intent around your competitors' products that you have to listen for and intervene early and often in those competitors' deal cycles. As marketers, we have more data than ever coming from these sources. So, how do you bring those silos of data generated from many apps in your marketing tech stack together to empower an SDR, or any salesperson, to have a meaningful interaction with a prospect or customer? You have to ingest, centralize, normalize, and organize all of that data into a single source of truth and then surface that to SDRs either through automation and action or through the visibility of dashboards and alerts.

SDRs and ABM: Absolute Alignment

If there's one connection that epitomizes absolute alignment between sales and marketing, it is the working relationship between SDRs and ABMs. At Snowflake, we deploy more of an account-based approach to how an SDR spends their time. It has been that way when sales development reported into sales and later when it transitioned to marketing. SDRs engage their ABM counterparts constantly to determine which marketing assets they will deploy to targeted prospects and customers based on those companies' purchasing intent.

There are good leads that come from demand gen campaigns that require follow-up. But the vast majority of an SDR's time is spent analyzing the behavior of new and existing accounts that could benefit from deploying our product. Which departments inside this account have been visiting our website, downloading content, and showing real propensity to buy? We bring those things together to empower an SDR to go after the right account at the right time, with the right message. SDRs work hand-in-glove with the account execs they support to proactively target companies at any specific time and in alignment with our sales strategy for any given month or quarter. This approach happens in tandem with ABM to deliver highly targeted campaigns to people in those accounts that are not yet known to us but who will eventually reveal themselves by responding to our marketing campaigns. It's more about the proactive motion. How do we get into a specific company, drive awareness into that organization, and then land and expand that customer? That's really where SDRs are focused outbound and where ABM plays a big role.

Related to this, the SDRs also work closely with their counterparts in our field marketing team. It all starts with where we want to get traction in any given quarter by deploying specific resources in those accounts. And the SDRs are right in the middle of that. The focus of our field marketing team is supporting account execs with local marketing events that SDRs can leverage in their highly targeted account-specific sales motions.

SDRs and Demand Generation

Demand gen by nature is broadly focused by vertical industry, product, and use case. It's serving a different function at the top of the funnel.

It's spreading awareness, picking up on interest in the market, and educating that interest at all times. And those leads can convert extremely fast into meetings and opportunities. Yet, demand gen is an engine that runs constantly, surfacing leads that are extremely good and valuable.

Today, demand gen is not just talking about responses, or even qualified responses. They frame their world in terms of the overlap they're having with the list of accounts that sales wants to talk to and sell to. Demand gen professionals are indexing, measuring, and in some cases paying themselves on the hit rate of their lead generation campaigns and events targeted at new and existing accounts that the sales team says are important and valuable. That alone is a paradigm shift from how most demand gen teams still work, which is everyone orienting around the customer and the accounts they've identified and placed in their customer relationship management (CRM) solution to track, pay attention to, and get to know. This all flows back to the day-to-day life of the SDRs, whose goal is to also help turn those leads into qualified prospects for account execs.

The Tech Stack SDRs Rely On

Snowflake deploys around 40 different sales and marketing SaaS technologies, including our own version of our product. From this, we get a single view of customers and the prospect companies we care about. That view is ultimately delivered to our end users—our SDRs. It's a sophisticated but purposeful tech stack. The true art of implementing and orchestrating that tech stack is unifying it so SDRs only need to know how to use three to four tools on a daily basis. For example, they can pull up a dashboard powered by Snowflake machine learning models that contains analysis about the propensity of which accounts in their territory are potential buyers, and what they want to buy. From there, the SDRs can connect to research and data collection tools by double-clicking on each of those companies to find the relevant personas and potentially influencers and buyers they should reach out to and what those folks have been up to.

The final piece is a sales engagement platform, which has all of the prescriptive resources—email templates, call scripts, social touches through LinkedIn, and more. Those resources are just for that specific industry that the targeted company belongs to and the specific product use case that we think is the best fit for that company, at any specific point in time. We're surfacing this information to the SDRs to help them focus and be really thoughtful about: "How does this company make money? What do they care about? What are the strategic initiatives they have going on?" And then to focus on the customer by having really valuable conversations as opposed to an SDR going in cold or spending exponentially more time trying to find this information on their own.

Which Sales Teams Should Your SDRs Support?

As we mentioned previously, Snowflake reorganized its sales organization into three tiers: Our commercial team focuses on smaller accounts and smaller deals that are indicative of high-velocity sales cycles and supported by our inside sales account execs. SDRs generally aren't needed to support this team. Those opportunities are simple enough that an account exec can manage their own prospecting and closing their own deals. Moving up a level is our enterprise sales team, which comprises the vast majority of Snowflake account execs. Each of these account execs will manage between 20 and 100 accounts. This is where SDRs engage and support most sales reps.

Then we have majors, the strategic segment of sales, which is very heavy with existing named accounts and big prospect accounts we want to pursue. That's a different motion where each account exec could have just one customer assigned to them based on its size. Historically, we've had looser SDR coverage on those accounts because it's just a different type of relationship. There are a lot more sales support people involved and many partner relationships in play. On the flip side of that, we have deployed one SDR to a single, huge account but mainly on developing new opportunities. For example, a massive customer has a number of subsidiaries. It has its own set of companies with different business interests that have different levels of market penetration. To assist, we execute a "pod model" in certain cases, where we over-invest in SDR support to go really deep and partner in a single, major account. What determines SDR involvement is the complexity of the account and whether or not the account exec has the bandwidth to uncover every opportunity on their own.

Metrics for SDR Success

A huge benefit of an account-based sales strategy is that you don't have the risk of SDRs spending time booking meetings with Joe's Bait and Tackle Shop. We're not focused on producing results in accounts that we're not explicitly targeting at any one time. The product of an SDR, first, is meetings. Within meetings, we track things like what percent of those meetings are with people who have director-plus titles. What is the current tech landscape of those meetings? What information did we uncover about the current state of that business and the pain points associated with it? That's all on the meetings front. Another key conversion point is how are those meetings converting into new opportunities as judged by the account exec? That's the critical handoff point. If the SDR team is delivering a bad product (i.e. bad meetings), then you'll see a low conversion rate to opportunities.

That's where your sales operations must intervene and coach the SDR, and realign them with their account execs. That conversion rate from meetings to opportunities is our key quality and efficiency metric. An opportunity is described as an account exec saying: "Yep, I've had a few meetings with this prospect. There's a real deal here. I'm engaged with the right people and there's a strong use case for Snowflake. I'm going to put this into my pipeline. I'm going to give it a forecasted close date, put a dollar amount on it and take ownership of next steps of a potential deal that I can close." We also monitor progression of those opportunities toward close. But these outcomes could play out over a six- to nine-month sales cycle that an account exec is driving. So, there's a huge dependence on the account exec and the team around them to go and win those deals. But we do pay attention to that from an SDR perspective to make sure they're impacting the business.

15

Scaling a Data-Driven Marketing Organization

"Surround yourself with people who know what you don't."
—Denise Persson

MARKETING HAS ALWAYS evolved in tandem with our sales organization. When Frank came onboard, we created industry-specific go-to-market motions. It was about aligning very much with the business needs and outcomes of customers. It's not just about your technology. You need to understand how technology relates to and solves the business problems your customers have. We developed these industry-specific offerings and marketing campaigns but we didn't do this on our own. We developed them with our business partners, who specialize in industry solutions. We expanded from marketing to just the technologist to the senior level personas on the business side of organizations.

Like our sales team, the marketing team had to grow and deliver on Snowflake's early revenue mantra of "triple, triple, triple, double, double." Your organizational paradigm has to shift often because you're absorbing resources so quickly. Snowflake's marketing team started with just eight people. Now we have more than several hundred in the organization. It's more challenging when you have to build such a structure while scaling so aggressively. As you hire more people, you create more functional teams. All the while, you have to scale efficiently to triple your lead flow each year, and then double it in later years. We faced the practical problem of hiring people, putting them into a structure that made sense so they knew what to do, and then having them execute incredibly fast but not at the expense of working people too hard.

Get Rid of the Hamsters

One problem a lot of startups encounter is that they achieve $10 million or $100 million in revenue relatively quickly and then their growth slows, because they rely too much on manual work. As discussed in Chapter 8, automation is a key pillar to a marketing team's scale and success. From early on, we all talked about automating the hamster work. You can't scale with hamsters. Entrenched competitors have infrastructure, market share, and more money to spend. Other startups want to beat you to every milestone and will deploy sound, and occasionally less-then-sound, go-to-market practices to get there. When you are scaling rapidly, you have to look at every component of your buyers' journeys and replace every time-consuming effort with procedures that are replicable. We invested a lot on the technical side to remove the barriers to automation. It was hugely expensive but it was worth it in the long run. Otherwise, we would have never succeeded in helping Snowflake get to, and beyond, $100 million in revenue.

Everything becomes about scale. If you can't scale it, you can't do it. Each marketing team needs platforms and technologies to automate those processes. In the early days, it's about people sending email requests. You can't do that anymore. In order to scale, you have to automate and track everything you do. I can't have people saying to me: "I need more people." You need to explain why. We even automated our brand and creative processes. Those teams started using a SaaS project management system. We started tracking inbound requests for everything. When we scale the team, we need to show numbers for that. We have to show why something is growing. You need to show that with data. So, you need systems to manage every single function to show why you need more people, or not.

You also need to automate to show more efficiencies. Especially in marketing, we can't grow with the size of the sales organization. You need to find efficiencies and add resources to where they're going to deliver the greatest marketing output and impact. Should you put 30 people on the brand and creative side or 30 people on the demand gen side? The tools and processes we use allow us to measure and make data-driven decisions on the right investment. Get rid of the hamsters and gain data-driven, operational efficiencies.

Establish Marketing Operations

In the beginning, we didn't yet have the resources to build and scale an internal operations team, so we worked with an outsourced team. Whether in-house or outsourced, operations are key to marketing campaign execution. Marketing ops handles project planning, marketing research, implementation, analyzing campaign performance, and data management. Yet, it became obvious within the first year that we needed more frequency. We were showing up to the sales team once a week or once a month with an avalanche of leads from events and campaigns we had run. Instead, we needed a constant flow of leads, so we moved operations in-house within a year. In response, our operations team grew in size to manage the growing number of apps we needed to automate functions and to conduct more sophisticated lead generation and ABM programs, while analyzing all of that data. The majority of these apps are chosen by your demand gen team. Other apps help automating processes across all other teams, such as product marketing, content marketing, PR, and those who manage your website.

Your operations team helps onboard and manage these apps, which often handle sensitive data. Before they can do that, your data security team must determine if each app complies with industry data security requirements. This can be an involved process, but it should also be automated so your security and operations teams can approve and deploy these SaaS apps with minimal input from the marketing teams that need to use them. Often, these apps are built to integrate with each other, or at least pass data from one to another. They each handle specific functions of identifying and serving prospects with highly targeted campaigns and then analyzing the performance of those campaigns along the customer journey.

The Modern Marketing Data Stack

More than 14,000 marketing technology solutions exist. You will need a few to get started and a few dozen to run a sizable marketing organization. All the while, you can't be inundated or stifled by the process to choose what works best for your organization. Snowflake produces an annual report that defines a number of martech categories that include many of these tools and solutions and the functions they automate in marketing and advertising, along with the data and AI technologies that underpin them. The Modern Marketing Data Stack report categorizes these solutions into analytics and data capture; data enrichment and hygiene; customer identity and onboarding; customer data platforms; marketing and customer engagement; programmatic solutions; and measurement and optimization technologies. Underpinning these technologies are data tools and platforms that focus on data integration and modeling; consent management; and business intelligence for data visualization. All of the data generated from these solutions should be in one place and used to create, deploy, and analyze your marketing programs.

The key takeaway from this methodology is that a single marketing solution, or a group of them, does not define your marketing strategy. Instead, determine what you will need in the beginning to quickly and efficiently create and deliver campaigns to generate a steady flow of quality leads. Have a plan in place to identify which additional martech solutions you will need six months in advance. The tech is there but you also need to have the skill sets internally to use the technology and bridge that technology with marketing business problems. You need to have data scientists on your marketing team. In many companies, data scientists are centralized away from marketing so they don't solve the business problems that marketing has. As your lead generation execution becomes more automated, then your need to deliver more sophisticated and targeted programs will increase. You can gain more detailed insights into why your marketing campaigns perform the way they do and how to hone the process of delivering the right messages to the right audiences at the right time, in real time.

Your Single, Integrated, and Automated Source of Truth

At prior companies, I wanted to know whether a marketing campaign was working or not, but too often my decisions were based on sophisticated guesses. It was normal to ask the IT department for data and then receive it three weeks later. The data was good but it was too late. In marketing, you have active campaigns and programs running. You need the ability to make changes in real time to see the biggest impact. We saw the potential of this for Snowflake as a customer-centric business. This was a complete game changer for us in marketing and sales.

The term "a single source of truth" in computing emerged more than half a century ago. For decades, software providers have featured the term prominently in their marketing. The features and technology to achieve this still contend with the growing pace at which new solutions emerge to help automate every part of a business. Marketing organizations still labor over achieving this elusive goal. It's what enables a similarly well-trodden term in our domain—customer 360—a complete profile of your customer based on all available data. Yet, most marketing intelligence teams remain disconnected from their companies' IT organizations despite marketing organizations' need to generate and acquire vast amounts of data.

At Snowflake, we made this a company-wide priority from the early days. At the same time, we had an advantage. We deployed our commercial product internally to achieve this. Nearly every app has the ability to store the data it generates in its own repository. That could work if you use just that one app. We use dozens of apps in marketing and that number continues to grow. They each serve a specific purpose to advancing our strategy, and they each generate data constantly. We bypass those individual repositories and also avoid pumping that data into a cloud-infrastructure repository with limited functionality. The silos that each of your martech solutions creates prevents having a single source of truth. Simple cloud storage makes it a challenge to derive significant value from your data. Strive for an automated process that stores all of your marketing data in a single and fully managed cloud data platform that provides efficient access from any location and enables all forms of business intelligence and the most advanced analytics possible. Whatever solution you choose, this should be your goal.

Sounds like a lot. Yet, it's just part of a much bigger picture. All of your sales data should be stored and integrated in your data platform, as well. In fact, all data from your finance, engineering, and other departments in your company should land there with near-zero manual effort to make this happen. And, of course, there is all of the data your SaaS product generates constantly about your customers' usage. We have functional data owners across all of these domains and who create data models that make it easy for all of our go-to-market teams to leverage data. At other companies I've worked for, the teams within those functions will only look at the data that they're using. That makes it very difficult to communicate to your counterparts on those other teams. Even sharing data seamlessly across functions could involve massive amounts of avoidable work from your IT department. We can share data with sales, for example, or have them build a core data model that we can reference easily. This is a fundamental differentiator for us. As your company grows and your efforts intensify, you will look for external data sources to enrich the data you generate internally for an even deeper knowledge of your customers, company, and the markets you serve. This is an always-evolving effort. Once set in motion, you will be able to reveal insights and accomplish things your competitors could only dream of.

Snowflake's data strategy allows us to ask in real time how people are responding to the campaigns we're running. Are we engaging with the right prospects? You can attract a lot of people with lofty titles, but are you drawing in the people you want to engage? If not, you can shut down a channel or adjust a campaign that isn't performing optimally and move that saved money to campaigns with bigger returns. Today, marketing is more about continuously optimizing. The more you can hyper-personalize something, the better results you're going to get. There are extremely sophisticated marketers out there who can do this. The companies that are winning today are those who can actually do that level of personalization and can get the most out of their marketing dollars. To be really successful, you will also do a lot of co-marketing with partners. With the right data, you can see which partners are truly helping to drive demand and those who aren't. Without data in real time, you will have money going into the wrong things, constantly. Even with AI moving forward in marketing, the basic ingredient to AI success is data. We will all encounter personalization with regard to content of all types. Videos will be completely generated with AI. It will be a whole different world out there. But it's a world based on data. With a single source of data, you can't fall back on marketing's old adage, "Half the money I spend (on marketing) is wasted. The trouble is I don't know which half." If you don't have the right data strategy, you might as well put sewer water in your car's gas tank.

Drink Your Own Champagne

We've stated previously how important it is to get customer feedback on your product. Chris did so before we had any customers. That process continued to snowball with our customer advisory board, the usage metrics we capture as a SaaS provider, the relentless pursuit of our sales reps to help our customers to gain continued value from our product, and the feedback from Snowflake sales engineers, professional service consultants, and partners. To truly catapult this effort to the next level, and if it makes sense, deploy your SaaS offering internally to help run your business. The more common term for this strategy is "eating your own dog food." The more business-friendly metaphor for this strategy is "drinking your own champagne."

Gaining input from customers is vital. Gaining insight from your product as a customer yourself is exceptional. You'll advance the pace at which you improve your product if your own business depends on it. The majority of SaaS providers report that they have a version of their product deployed internally. Why, and to what end? Is it just sitting there so the provider can make that claim? Does it operate on the fringes? Or, is it a mission-critical solution that, if it failed, your business would halt? The higher the risk, then the higher the reward.

In addition, customers are more confident if a vendor relies heavily on the product it sells. Your marketing team can develop champagne campaigns that highlight the value your company derives from internal use. More importantly, your marketing efforts can reveal the use cases that your product addresses across your business. Use cases that your customers haven't even thought of but see massive value from as they consider how your product can reveal new opportunities down the road. Customers learning from other customers is essential to the success of a SaaS company. But customers who agree to participate in your marketing efforts can only reveal so much about their business for competitive reasons. Also, you can't bombard those customers often with multiple marketing campaign requests. When you're the customer, you can reveal what you want and how often. Who better to push your product to new frontiers and market those use cases than the customer who knows the product better than anyone else on the planet?

It was always our intention to use our product to help run our company. We wanted to use machine learning and AI in marketing. A key use case for us in marketing was learning how to predict our sales pipeline. On the marketing side in many B2B companies, when it comes to pipeline management, you always find out too late. Most marketing teams only realize in the middle of a quarter that a region doesn't have enough pipeline. Finding out at the beginning of a quarter is also too late. Marketing can't do anything by then to increase or accelerate pipeline to impact revenue in a current quarter. Using AI to predict today how much pipeline we will need to be successful in six months is a game changer.

Make Your Customers Incredibly Happy

Gone are the days of sales reps doing everything a customer asks right up until they sign a deal, and then disappearing immediately to chase the next opportunity. At Snowflake, we ran with the concept that our customers are our product marketers. They define the product. We tell their story, tell it loudly and enable our sales reps to get these stories out. That's better than a founder or CEO saying publicly "I love this product" or getting a celebrity to do the same. You need your customers to endorse your product. We maximize customer happiness because people don't necessarily trust sales people and their marketers. They trust their peers, so we let those peers do the marketing. Our customers couldn't stop talking about our product and how well we treat them. Our team would set up video shoots at our user conferences with customers, asking them for a testimonial. We would have a line out the door. It's influencer marketing at its best. Looking back, the market's awareness of Snowflake was the result of thousands of customers talking about us each and every day. Unfortunately, this is far from normal.

Most customers don't want to endorse their software vendors. Typically, there is a gap between what the customer was promised and the actual functionality and value available from the product. This has been happening ever since the software industry emerged. That creates a huge opportunity for the startup that positions their product accurately, gets their customers up and running quickly, and continues to deliver value throughout a long business relationship.

Create and Scale Additional Marketing Teams

In Chapter 7, we detailed the core teams needed to jump-start your marketing organization—demand generation, public relations, and content, customer, field, and partner marketing teams. In this chapter, we've discussed the importance of adding or growing teams beyond a single person—marketing operations and marketing intelligence. There are other teams that are integral to your success early on, and later when your company and your marketing team scales and evolves.

Product Marketing

We've talked about the importance of a demand-gen-led marketing team when you hire your first sales and marketing professionals. But that doesn't mean product marketing shouldn't happen then, as well. Early on, certain teams within marketing are more challenging to hire for. It can take a while to find the right person to lead product marketing. But that didn't stop us from marketing our product each and every day back then. We were a small company and everyone pitched in when anyone else needed their help. Bob Muglia and our founders, engineers, sales engineers, and marketers with technical backgrounds all pitched in to hone our message. Our content team was in lockstep with them to produce great product content. Whether you have a head of product marketing or not, you should be able to tap the expertise of the experts already inside your small startup.

Product marketing in a startup transforms as often as the startup itself. Repositioning Snowflake from the "data warehouse built for the cloud" to the "cloud data platform" was an absolute imperative to install leadership and structure for this team. When we did, it exploded (in a good way). We structured the team to cover the different technologies that comprise our product and the use cases that our product enables. From there, we expanded by hiring people who managed featured capabilities that our cloud-built data platform inspires, such as customers developing applications on top of our product, and our marketplace that features third-party data and AI products that customers and prospects can trial and purchase.

As your product evolves, you need product marketing specialists who can focus on specific domains within your product. Among many functions, these marketers work with your product management team to understand what new product features and functions are coming. From there, they draft detailed messaging that explains these forthcoming innovations, what problems they address, what opportunities they create, who are the targeted personas of this messaging, and which of your competitors play in this space and how their offerings compare. Once finalized, these marketers provide that messaging to your sales organization and update existing sales tools and develop new ones. This messaging also informs all of the related product content that appears in all forms and is delivered from the rest of your marketing organization, including your website.

Our product marketing team also includes our vertical/industry marketing. As we've mentioned earlier, your success depends on knowing when to pivot from solely marketing to technical professionals. Eventually, you will have to widen your strategy by messaging how your product addresses the larger business problems and opportunities of your customers. This messaging has to go further to address the business of specific industry verticals. Talking to the vice president of product development in a healthcare company is very different from a conversation with an executive at a retail giant. They care about very different things.

When we made this shift, we grouped verticals into tiers and focused first on the top tier by developing messaging in stride with the sales team as they hired industry-specific sales and consulting experts. Early in this book, we discussed how gaming and ad tech companies were our early bread-and-butter customers. But that strategy was not an industry focus. It was a technology focus. Those companies were most likely to adopt our product based on their digital strategy and data needs. We still market to those industries, but they were not part of the first tier of vertical marketing and sales strategies. They weren't the largest industries we eventually chose to target, but they're still very important to us. Our first industry targets included financial services, healthcare and life sciences, retail and consumer goods, advertising/media/entertainment, and the public sector. Within product marketing, we hired professionals who either had previous experience marketing to each of these industries or were hungry to learn about them. If you never venture beyond marketing the technical benefits of your product, you'll never experience the growth and success of evolving from a startup to a global technology powerhouse.

This team started to really evolve in time for our inaugural user conference in 2019 and every year thereafter. We've state previously that your product marketing team will own all or nearly all of this week-long event. It's all hands on deck to prepare the event that embodies everything about your company. If you continue to innovate your technology offerings and continue to scale every part of your business, your user conference will grow in size from a few thousand attendees annually to more than ten thousand in just a few years. It's a global event that brings together customers, prospects, and partners, where your product and executive teams announce new product capabilities, host dozens or hundreds of technical and business sessions, and arrange meetings for all of your company's stakeholders to meet and discuss the value of your technology and relationships.

Community and Developer Marketing

To make your product sticky and make yourself a long-term partner, you must capture the hearts and minds of the people who comprise your user and developer communities. They can represent your customers, prospects, partners, and others who use or are trialing your product and need help leveraging it to fit their technical and business use cases. Provide technical content, such as sample code that your community needs and from people whom they trust and respect. Use these introductory touchpoints to build a conversation and a relationship with these people for the long term. It's a community, not just a one-and-done. They have to be part of something bigger.

Snowflake's community is about 800,000 people, as of this writing. It's substantial and it's growing quickly. The number of communities that we can help be successful in this new era of generative AI has grown exponentially. Our job is to make sure we understand the needs of each of our communities. For example, a community of Python developers looks different than a community of Snowflake developers, which looks different than a Kubernetes community. Understand the patterns of your communities and bring in the right people who understand each one and can present ways for these communities to get their jobs done, better and faster.

These experts should be able to tell stories backed by very specific code samples that address problems in very credible and meaningful ways. It's not just marketecture. Your team that manages your community should understand the problems people are looking to solve and how they want to grow their capabilities. It's about creating the narrative around this and then creating very hands-on, how-to technical content for people to use, and being there to help answer questions as people in your communities run into difficulties. Then, your community team should think about how to take the content your team is building, or your community experts create, and deliver it to your community members.

Reach into those communities and tell them a story that doesn't lead with your product or services but with the scenarios and the problems your community members are trying to address. As much as possible, speak to them in a more agnostic perspective. But there will be plenty of opportunities to use your product to efficiently solve their problems, and that's okay. Just make sure you deliver value they can act on and not marketing-speak that will turn them away. In that realm, recommending they sign up for a trial of your product (if they haven't already) is okay. During this whole process, don't differentiate between customers and broader community members. They all just want to learn what's going on. If you get somebody to learn something that matters to them and you establish credibility, that engagement allows you to start a conversation with them.

The content you deliver to a user or developer community is often a combination of free structured learning delivered by an expert. Connect developers with the person who has created that content so they're not just learning from you. It's about an individual expert teaching people. The next thing is building out content packages of blog posts and videos. All roads should lead back to something tangible, such as a code-based object that people can start using very quickly. It's a very efficient path if the sample codes are available in super familiar and accessible ways. Also, take that code on the road and present it at your events designed for communities or at third-party conferences. Interactive environments are key.

To attract your community to events, you'll need the help of your demand gen team to market community-specific webinars or an invitation to your developers conference. Your community and developer relations group can work with demand gen to develop highly targeted and credible content. It's much more authentic and direct from somebody they respect. Work with demand gen to help nurture attention and draw your communities to events. From there, start building these learning journeys but also capture the data about how these communities engage with your content. Then partner with demand gen about the next topic for your community to learn. This impacts how you craft content and determines what your communities should do next to grow their capabilities that benefit them personally and professionally.

Partner with demand gen to also get communities to trial your product. As they use it, they will generate signals within the product that help demand gen understand which features they're using. This is how you bridge community with sales. If you know 20 people from a customer are using a specific feature very heavily, you can alert your salesperson responsible for that account. A lot of growth in trials at Snowflake comes from our developer community.

The big intangible goal here is to make every person feel that your product is for them. "They understand me. They work with the languages I use. There are resources to help me learn new things quickly, and they allow me to do something with applications that I couldn't do before." This is a long-term journey but you want your communities to feel that your community and developer teams understand them, and that your product helps them get their jobs done better and faster.

Brand Marketing

Establishing your brand early on is a must. You will likely accomplish this with a creative agency before you establish this function in-house. Your messaging is susceptible to many factors and is expected to change slightly a number of times during your startup years, and beyond. But your brand is here to stay. You may make minor tweaks over time but your brand is what distinguishes your company and sets it apart when people experience your website or one of your marketing campaigns for the first time. Continuity is key, especially as your marketing team expands and your programs and campaigns spread across all channels and geographies.

Your brand means something, too. It represents your company, culture, mission, and values. So, take the time to understand what your brand should look like. The right creative agency should take you through a process that leaves you confident the brand you chose will last forever. It should also reflect how you want your customers, your business ecosystem, and the broader market to perceive you. And, it should separate you from your competitors in a way that tells your communities how your company stands apart. Your brand isn't just colors and shapes that seem cool. It has to fuse with your messaging as well. If your company tone is informative, insightful, disruptive, or a combination of elements, so should be your brand.

Once you exit the process to develop your brand, and all of your relevant stakeholders have provided their input and approval, you need to cement your brand with company-wide guidelines. It's easy for teams far from your headquarters to produce prospect-facing content without regard to brand continuity. Stop this before it starts. Develop company-wide brand guidelines and make them available to everyone. Most often, when your brand is compromised, it's not intentional. Your teams far from home need your help. Otherwise, they will produce content quickly for good reason, such as a live sales event, but that doesn't align with your brand. Without guidelines, they're not to blame. And always make your external agency, and later on your in-house team, available for quick feedback whenever someone in the field has questions.

When you do have the resources to hire a brand team, keep it tight for a while. You will always need brand folks to come up with a new but consistent design element to promote an event or develop new templates. At the same time, your brand team will spend as much time protecting your existing brand as they will extending it to new endeavors.

Executive Communications

Creating this team could be a few years, or more, after you launch your startup. For a while, your only spokesperson will be your founder or CEO. Hopefully, they will have an established reputation and will garner a lot of attention when participating in your marketing endeavors. Knowing that, your head of content and head of PR or communications can ably manage your executive comms, with your CMO as the executive resource. As we mentioned earlier in this book, our first CEO Bob Muglia was a "yes" for everything we asked him to do. Of course, we had him promote and participate in only the most crucial events. Working with individual executives on the topics that are dear to their hearts is key. As you scale, it's not possible to have just your CEO as the face of marketing or your only executive sales influencer. Your whole leadership team needs to be executive sponsors. Most of our executive team made themselves available to sales and marketing, helping advance Snowflake's go-to-market strategy in vertical industries and horizontal lines of business.

When Frank arrived, he impressed upon his direct reports that they should all be involved in sales opportunities that would benefit from their experience. If a prospect was considering Snowflake as the backbone of the finance and accounting, then our CFO should make themselves available to support that opportunity. The same went for all of our domain experts at the highest levels in Snowflake. We in marketing also saw that as an opportunity. Over a period of a year, we set in motion a program to bolster our executives' thought leadership by elevating their prominence in the market or leveraging the prominence they established before joining Snowflake. But you have to tread lightly if you want them to participate. If they say "no," that's more about the marketing team and less about the executive. Most want to help, but you have to accomplish three things in order to gain their approval.

First, you have to prove to them their time will be well spent. Specifically, their participation will deliver great value to the company in the way of garnering large readership, attracting positive media coverage, and attracting new customers. Second, you have to raise at least one of their eyebrows. These are brilliant people who have done great things throughout their careers. They are also incredibly informed. For example, if you propose an interview or a blog post with a view on a topic that's been written about widely by others, or is outside their own domain, they're going to understandably shut the door on you. Third, they will halt everything the moment they realize you've engaged them in any part of the process that is better suited for someone further down their management chain. These are not easy hurdles to overcome but they're not impossible, either. You have to nail down all of these before you can think about asking.

Case in point: Before we had an executive comms person or team, we decided it was time to get our executives talking about what they know best. Specifically, we wanted to showcase what their departments were doing at Snowflake that most other companies weren't. We kicked off a year-long blog strategy. We proposed to each senior executive about doing a series of three blogs over a six-week period. To save them time, we first approached one or two of their direct reports who knew the mind of their executive in order to determine which topics were most important to them. Then, we continued to work with those direct reports to develop detailed outlines for each blog. When we did get each executive into their interviews, they spent 40 minutes on each occasion. If they touched on insightful topics but understandably didn't have supporting details, we interviewed their direct reports, who helped us at the outset, to fill in the gaps. We also chose a specific order for which executives we would approach first. We started with our CIO, who was known to be very approachable. He also happened to report to our CFO, which is common in many companies. We used our success with the CIO as proof that our CFO would not waste his time with the same endeavor. From there, most of our executives participated in a blog series, which all turned out to be incredibly successful.

There will come a time when you will need someone to engage your executives beyond ad hoc requests and develop a strategy and execution plan for executive communications. While your startup is still growing, this could be your head of PR. Or, you could hire a person responsible for exec comms. Either way, this person must have experience successfully running such programs for a number of years. And they have to be incredibly thoughtful and aware when engaging senior executives with requests that the execs will see as important to the company. Otherwise, your exec comms person will get the thumbs-down from your CEO and others on their team very quickly. Once that happens, you will have limited marketing access to your executives, who are left wondering why the person you chose to engage them fell short of their expectations early on in that role.

Establish Cross-Functional Teams

As your marketing organization grows and evolves, you will need to further align the teams within marketing to best support your sales organization and your customers. Meetings that reoccur with the same people for the same projects are not as effective as aligning individuals from multiple teams to have sole responsibility for a specific go-to-market strategy.

Marketing, including at Snowflake, is still organized by traditional functions. But it doesn't stay just that way when developing 6- or 12-month strategies and executing on those strategies. A prospect's or customer's experience of your marketing is the result of work from people across multiple teams. You're not impinging on the traditional structure of the organization. To deliver effective outcomes, you have to create cross-functional operational teams. For example, if you wanted to create a demand generation program targeting specific individuals in the manufacturing industry, you would create a team that would include a member from the product marketing industry team, along with someone from content marketing, demand generation, public relations, ABM, and anyone else needed to envision, create, and deliver that program. At Snowflake, we designate such people from each functional group in marketing to own programs as a cross-functional team that serves each of our targeted vertical industries, horizontal business functions, and the data workloads and featured capabilities that comprise our product technology.

This is a much more powerful strategy than assembling groups of marketers only when the need arises. At least four times a year, these go-to-market teams plan their programs and campaigns months ahead of time and inform the other teams. They base their schedule on a number of influencing factors, such as the sonic boom events that our marketing organization as a whole plans each year, industry and technology events known to occur on a regular schedule, and the constant flow of insights coming from the marketing and sales data stored in our data platform. Every member of the team becomes an expert about the industry or workload for which they're responsible, so they can continue to deliver innovative programs. In the early days, we had each marketer participating in multiple cross-functional teams because the number of your target markets will almost certainly grow. To cover them all, you will need all hands on deck. This still happens today.

16

Going Global

"Don't go global until you hit $100 million in US annual revenue."
—Chris Degnan

THE BIG CUSTOMERS who bet big on us during Snowflake's startup phase were forward-thinking, desperate, or a combination of both. They saw that our product was in line with their technology and business visions, such as going all in on cloud computing. Or, their current technology was inhibiting the customer experience, stifling company growth and ruling the lives of their IT people. These were customers that wouldn't normally bet on a startup, especially one that's barely GA and offers an enterprise solution that would be at the center of their entire data strategy. Nearly all of them required enhancements to our product—new features and functionality that appeal to many customers, satisfy the product requirements of industries that we were not yet ready to sell to, and would not require unfathomable demands upon our engineering team. This deviation from our plan of selling to smaller companies in one or two specific industries was not constrained to our customers in the United States. There were plenty of big companies abroad that were already in our current target markets.

There was some interest in whether we should go into Europe at this point. Of course, that would start with the United Kingdom. Countries where English is spoken most often are the first targets of expansion for

US-based growing startups. John McMahon recommended that we "hold (off) as long as you can," because it's expensive and painful, in all sorts of ways. So, we really focused on building the major markets in the United States first—New York City, Boston, Seattle, San Francisco—the list went on. We would hire reps in regions where we saw significant growth early in Snowflake's history. This approach cascaded down to the regional sales managers who we eventually hired. The people we first hired were grinders. They loved to jump-start new markets for us. We targeted the East and West Coasts, then focused on building the central United States. Because Snowflake is a cloud-only solution, the Midwest developed at a slower pace for us. Organizations headquartered in that region were slower to adopt and eventually migrate to the cloud. When it came to landing and expanding in EMEA and Asia Pacific and Japan (APJ) we took a measured approach.

How It Starts: The Pull Effect

The initial stage is pure response mode. Companies abroad heard about us on their own. We had no marketing campaigns happening outside the United States. For most startups, it's just your website, current customers that had footholds in other countries, and word of mouth. Snowflake had one other aspect to unsolicited demand—digital-native companies. They were often startups, like us, and were solely focused on cloud solutions to build and run their businesses. One of our SDRs was selling into an online food delivery company in Europe. We could see the physical pain on the customers' faces during our video conference calls with them. The company was using a competitor's product and suffering in a material way. We sold into that company before we had any boots on the ground in Europe. From there, we dedicated an inside sales rep in Silicon Valley to cover interest from Europe that was coming our way without a demand gen strategy.

As interest grew, John said, "You're going to hire someone in London. It's the center of the (European) universe, it's English-speaking and Snowflake doesn't have any translation capabilities yet." As more of those deals came up for us, we hired our first head of EMEA sales in 2017. He was based in London, multilingual, and had held sales management roles in multinational technology firms prior to Snowflake. France and Germany were our next targets, so this made sense. We were very deliberate about going into those countries. The people up in the Nordics, the Swedes in particular, are early adopters. But again we were very reactive to it until they pulled us in. We hired someone similarly in Australia to cover Asia Pacific and Japan (APJ), who had also held such roles across that region. That was our first market in Asia, for a period of time. Again, we started with an English-speaking country. From there, we ventured into Singapore and then Japan, which can be a tough market to break into. We built the sales and marketing teams. The groups that supported them came later, while we established marketing and sales teams in other countries in those regions. Startups that spend big early on in other countries before they have any substantial revenue risk shutting down those operations even faster.

Get Ready to Spend, Not Reap

When do you do this as a company? If you attempt to do it too early, you're taking resources from North America, where you're super productive in terms of sales and marketing. You will have to invest in countries that won't be very productive at the beginning. Snowflake is very strong in the United States but we're still just scratching the surface. Yet, we also recognized that we needed to expand our service into Europe, APJ and beyond, because there is so much opportunity. With telcos, for example, there's only two or three big companies in each country. But when we land those, they can become huge customers. The percentage of growth internationally will naturally be higher year to year. But you have to be careful. It's expensive to expand into a new country or region. Initially, your people aren't as productive because you need to hire and train them. And the sales efficiencies will be lower in the beginning. It can take years to achieve the same level of efficiency that you have in the United States, where it is an endless market in terms of technology. The international market isn't as big.

We hired leaders who had done that job once or twice before. Often, you hire a leader who might have some UK sales experience but they understand all of Europe or all of APJ. So, the people we got were high-caliber leaders who really knew how to get started and succeed.

Also, we were really invested in their success. We didn't hire people and leave them. For example, we did our "Power Up Japan" video conference call every single week. We had their backs. Whatever they needed, we were there to help them. We weren't going to permanently vacate the offices in Japan, even though we started there just before the Covid pandemic. Our first hire there attended college in the United States. He would let us know about the problems and had a good ability to forecast deals. Once traction picked up, we hired our head of APJ, who was Canadian born but fluent in Japanese and had been a senior tech executive in APJ for more than a decade prior to Snowflake. We've been very deliberate about our approach. We haven't walked out of a market yet. Latin America has been a slower uptake for us due to instability of governments. More recently, we have launched in China and the Middle East.

Your Ideal Customer Profile

This was no different than our initial strategy in the United States or the United Kingdom. We had to sell to digital-native companies in the United Kingdom. Ironically, some of the earliest and largest customers were delivery services providers. We didn't even have a sales team in the United Kingdom at the time but we sold to these companies. In India and in Singapore, it has been the same. Those delivery services were the points of entry for us into those markets. If you have aspirations to sell to one of the biggest banks in the United Kingdom as one of your first 50 customers in Europe, good luck with that. You might get lucky. It's not impossible and I'm sure it's happened, but it's really hard. Use your ideal customer profile (ICP) that launched your sales strategy in the United States as your recipe over and over again when you launch in a new country. A lot of prospects in traditional companies in these countries have been in their jobs for years and don't want to leave. There's no benefit to them for taking risks. The digital-native companies, they're risk takers. Once you have a bunch of them as customers, one of your product champions in those companies eventually goes to a job in a traditional company. All of a sudden, "boom!," you're in. You just have to create this ecosystem of local, referenceable customers. That's your focus each and every time.

Deploying Abroad and Getting It Right

There's hardly a growth-oriented US company today that isn't excited by the opportunity to sell abroad. APJ alone includes about half of the world's population and three of the largest economies in the world—China, Japan, and India. However, breaking into these markets offers no shortage of challenges, including the multitude of languages, a highly differentiated economic and business landscape, and varying levels of market maturity and technology adoption. There's no one-size-fits-all playbook, and US companies often struggle deciding where to invest and what kind of ROI to expect. Despite these inherent challenges, EMEA and APJ continue to tempt companies because they offer a staggering opportunity for growth and financial success, if you get it right.

So, how do you get it right? You invest in the right teams in the right countries at the right time. You treat these regions as ongoing and evolving projects that take years to build. You reassess constantly where the best opportunities are, and adjust your priorities. And you drive success while educating and collaborating with your US headquarters on how to do business in these regions.

The key for Snowflake is our localized approach. Companies tend to focus on market expansion, hiring people, landing lighthouse accounts and referenceable customers, and closing business to justify more growth and opening more offices. Everyone's hustling in the same direction for about four to five years. However, once you reach 300–500 people in each region, you often find that this strategy has resulted in a centralized APJ office in Singapore or an EMEA office in the United Kingdom, with employees who are purely English speakers, and the addition of a management layer to increase support across functions. While this plan adds, in theory, more internal reporting and discussions that justify a bigger team in these two regions, there's an obvious issue: You're not investing in greater EMEA and APJ.

How can you possibly provide strong coverage across these vast regions, develop local relationships, and have a direct impact on countries when you aren't actually in the countries or speaking their languages? Simply put, it's impossible. The best strategy is to go local. The three key elements for success are to build teams that work locally, speak the local language, and understand the local business practices.

Drive behaviors from the field in response to what local customers want and need. Create an expansion plan that takes into account each market's maturity and evolves to match conditions by understanding market forces within each country.

In practice, that equates to building local organizations quickly as you enter each country. The first hire in an APJ country is your general manager (GM), which is the most crucial role. That person must hire local people and figure out how to sell your technology, set up order forms, and get partners and resellers signed up. It's a total startup environment where your GM is running the show and determining how best to localize. Everybody who works in that local organization is hands-on and rolling up their sleeves to meet and support customers.

It's important to treat each region or country as a distinct geography—not as a sales outpost but as an actual company with a GM leader who hires a head of sales, a head of marketing, a head of services, and a head of business strategy (BS). These organizations must be self-sufficient and engage directly with customers and partners. A lean APJ model is the best approach. Investing in localization helps you get the most impact and reduces reporting that springs from a large corporate APJ office. Investment is pushed out into the field, and APJ leaders are empowered to drive action. After all, they are the experts and know how to do business in their country.

The same strategy holds for EMEA, with one exception. The countries that comprise the EU, specifically your first targets, can be jump-started with a local sales rep and sales engineer. Marketing support for these countries can happen from the United Kingdom, initially. Once you build a significant pipeline, close deals on a consistent basis, and gain market traction overall, you can justify a country manager. Middle East and African nations resemble more the APJ model and need a GM as the first pair of boots on the ground. Of course, you don't want to recreate the wheel from a technology or sales perspective, so you should leverage all the great things that have happened in the company. Your organizations abroad should leverage best practices from your HQ and other global offices, and combine with their local team's knowledge to sell and support effectively in their country.

What It Takes to Succeed Abroad

Opening your business in any country is going to be a deep learning experience. If you follow the traditional path and start in the United Kingdom for EMEA, and Singapore, Australia, or New Zealand for APJ, it will give you a chance to get your footing, drive some early revenue, and strategize for the rest of the region. The key is to learn from each new market experience and build an expansion strategy that's based upon those learnings. Snowflake applied our learnings from building in Australia to speed up our Japan organization, which in turn sped up Korea based on new insights from Japan. We did the same once we set up shop in the United Kingdom. We transferred those learnings to other large economies, such as Germany, France, and the Nordics. This build-and-learn process produces a standard model that's smooth and effective in how we justify opening in a new country, how we build that initial team, how many people we need, what functions must be covered, and what kind of localization and marketing budgets we start with in order to gain traction quickly.

When it's time to start or expand in EMEA and APJ, you want to keep a number of factors in mind. Each country's GM must be a builder. Ideally, this person has a strong background and a record of success in the country, and has established relationships with C-suite leaders at big companies. You want somebody who has the presence of a local executive. He or she should be capable of scheduling conversations with high-level executives at companies, without requiring the presence of your CEO in order to get the meeting. Look for builders who have the presence and personality to access people significantly above them in terms of responsibility and numbers. This capability will drive bigger and better opportunities in the market, and your strategic engagement with customers will become much stronger. From day one, this person must have a startup mindset and behave like a GM.

A salesperson who simply closes deals in the EU makes sense for a short period of time. But a GM must have the DNA to get things done, escalate quickly to get things fixed, and can explain to HQ that, in order to do business, you must customize and localize. Execution and delivery are key. Good GMs don't simply paint a picture for the next three to five years of the kind of organization they want to build. They deliver startup-level growth on a quarterly basis to justify the investment they're looking for long term. Snowflake's primary hiring criteria is to find someone who has built businesses before and wants to roll up their sleeves and do it again. A person who has taken something from scratch, made it big, and loves the building phase. The GM must be willing to do everything from hiring, to sales, to briefing media and analysts, and establishing a culture within their own teams.

Hiring Locally

Local hires should be a group of people who hustle, have grit, and fit your culture. The base hiring criteria in non–native English countries is that everyone must be at least bilingual. They need to speak English for your global network and company, but they must also speak the local language. Over time, having everyone speak English becomes less relevant but it is crucial at the start. With a strong localization strategy, it's important for your GM to have the ability to hit the ground running and hire the right people immediately. The smart move is to provide headcount for coverage in every important role, from pre-sales to post-sales, starting on day one, and to put trust in the local experts.

Go-to-Market Approach

The startup opportunity abroad is very similar to adoption trends in the United States. You'll generally find that whatever happened in the United States with adoption trends will likely happen in EMEA and APJ. The same customer challenges will be solved, and the same value will be derived from your product. Snowflake saw early US adoption by cloud-native companies such as online marketing, ad tech, gaming, online media, and startup companies. Enterprises, large organizations, and financial services firms took longer because they have on-premises legacy solutions that require lengthy migrations and clearing of regulatory hurdles.

The same evolution happens abroad where a lot of our initial customers are cloud-native startups that shift over to Snowflake easily. As we gain traction in each market and our reputation solidifies, we engage in deeper business conversations with C-suite customers.

With that said, early customer deals are a lot of work. Set expectations during this initial land grab: Deliver a proof of concept for customers who don't know you and probably won't make a huge investment. However, these first customers pay for localization and enable you to hire more people. Once you have successfully onboarded customers, acquired some reference logos, and developed a reputation in the country, the deal sizes start to get bigger. The customer conversations change from technical benefits to a business discussion.

Partners

The United States is generally a direct customer model. You build a solution, customers try it, they like it, and then start using it. All of your internal systems and the way you sell and price are based on a direct sales model. Yet, partners are key to expanding your salesforce and your influence. In other countries, partner-influenced deals and product deployments led by systems integrators can be more significant than in the United States. Major companies in every industry—manufacturing, pharmaceutical, public sector, telecommunications—outsource data decisions, infrastructure management decisions, and application development to systems integrators or other third parties. Knowing this, if you try to go directly to customers in such countries, that won't work. To get traction with enterprises, you need to both sell the vision to the end user while selling the tech to partner companies, which means getting them on board and excited about your technology so they encourage sales to customer enterprises. Your sales model will need to be tweaked and partner programs improved to reflect this reality.

Bilateral Communication

Let your local leaders figure out the best way to sell your products. There is no one-size-fits-all. Engage your corporate HQ on what is working, what isn't, and how customers and partners are using your technology. This allows for sharing best practices to other parts of the world and influencing your road map on a global scale. The same goes for your teams of local people. Encourage them to interact with each other across regions. You want to create a cross-pollination effect of best practices across EMEA and APJ that speeds growth.

Have a Data-Driven Plan

Your plan for a region should be an evolving road map that takes into account market factors such as population density, potential customer density, gross domestic product, economic power, and geopolitical issues. When you're opening a new office, you need to know what sales pipeline growth looks like and how to staff a market. The best strategy is to build your APJ and EMEA plans using data and analytics. As much as possible, you want to remove the emotion and personalities from making decisions about what to do next and let the data speak for itself. When the company can see the data-driven decision-making involved and understand the size of the opportunity, you are more likely to get financial support and be able to launch a more aggressive plan successfully.

Advance Your Product Faster with a Presence in EMEA and APJ

Without question, EMEA and APJ represent exciting opportunities for tech companies, but you must take a localized approach. These regions are rife with opportunity to enhance your offering because different countries will test your solution in new ways. These markets will show you how to make your solution more robust and will reveal where you have hiccups. You may also find that you'll kick the tires on new functionality faster because of the distinct nature of the markets, and the scale at which you'll be receiving feedback. The demands of EMEA and APJ customers will make your solution better over time and expose new business practices, new ideas, and new partnerships you haven't seen before, but only if you take a localized approach and truly learn from these markets.

When and How to Verticalize Abroad

First and foremost, a verticalized sales motion helps deliver an enriched sales experience for your target customers. Your person standing in front of them knows their market, understands what they need, and can speak to how a solution will benefit them specifically. This sales rep is speaking their language and also connecting the dots between the solutions available and the challenges the customer faces in order to demonstrate the real benefits and outcomes they can expect.

An obvious challenge in EMEA and APJ are the multitude of countries and languages at play. However, it's important to recognize that verticalization also has its own language. In many ways, industries represent more of a shift in thinking than location. Some industries are more conservative, while others are more hierarchical, and sometimes cultural differences are layered on top of these two factors. So, hire local experts who ensure you interact and conduct business appropriately on every level.

One Size Does Not Fit All

There are two forces at play here. First, you should verticalize as soon as you can, assuming you have enough people to support this motion without damaging the rest of your business. Start with verticalizing your core markets fully and your secondary markets as much as possible. Yet, it's wise to hold off on any new markets with small teams until it's both feasible and desirable. Overall, verticalization abroad is not a one-size-fits-all action and depends on a multitude of factors:

1. **Solution.** The first consideration is what you're selling. For example, specific IT solutions (traditional infrastructure, application performance monitoring solutions) won't benefit much from applying industry-specific use cases. However, if you're selling a vision and a product that changes the way business is done across different types of companies and industries, then you will want to tailor sales to suit vertical customers.
2. **Market maturity.** Companies that are new to a market or launching a new product will usually need to evangelize the solution first. The focus is on finding a market fit and selling products quickly, which doesn't open up the ability to dive deeply into an industry. In general, verticalization is a better strategy for more established companies.
3. **Sales reps.** Young companies or those launching in new markets are also unlikely to have enough sales reps. Even larger companies will need to establish an on-ground presence in a country or region if they want to verticalize properly. Numbers matter. If you must hire an entire team while verticalizing, you will face an uphill challenge.

4. **GTM strategy.** If your target buyers have different challenges or needs across industries, then verticalization can help you to better position and sell your solution. Again, if you are selling a product that works the same no matter what company uses it, then verticalization makes no sense. It takes much more effort to message and position a verticalized solution, so you want to use your resources wisely.
5. **Total addressable market.** From a planning perspective, you need to look at where you already have a footprint and a mass of sales reps to make a logical movement. Look at the total addressable market by industry and by region. Can you generate enough revenue in a specific market to justify such a sales motion?
6. **Partner-led markets.** Some EMEA and APJ markets are too remote and should remain partner-driven areas. There's no reason to sell directly to those markets or verticalize them because partners have more experience and can better manage the sale.

Take Advantage of Pilot Programs

Consider running a pilot program in one country and for one vertical before rolling out to an entire region. We conducted a pilot by creating a financial services sales team in the United Kingdom. We picked a vertical with a high concentration of target customers, a known market need, the ability to hire industry experts with ease, and lots of great research and information to consume in order to understand that vertical. Our pilot program allowed the entire team to see how vertical sales work, empowered us to work out any kinks with operationalizing our strategy, and helped us determine how to best scale verticalization across the region.

To launch a pilot, look for the most logical and easiest test ground possible where lots of opportunity exists. That requires examining each country you want to be in, understanding what verticals are strongest, and assessing the overall aptitude to adopt technology. This analysis not only helps with selecting a pilot location but will also be useful when you plan and roll out verticalization across EMEA and APJ.

Use Data to Define Your Strategy

Any company that sells horizontally today has amassed data around customer sales. We recommend using data from your CRM to help make sense of which places to verticalize based on what your customers are doing today, what the pipeline looks like going forward, and what industries jump out as hotbeds for you. You may also want to couple this data with external market data to validate where opportunities might exist. And, of course, listen to anecdotal data points from your sales reps. They are on the ground and often know best.

Provide Good Sales Enablement

Everyone on your team must understand why verticalization matters and how it will make sales reps more successful. To help with the transition and enablement, hire industry experts. In addition, create sales enablement training and materials that explain how verticalization works, provide industry knowledge and language, educate sales reps on the use cases of a specific vertical, and explain how to sell the solution in that context. In addition, it's critical to encourage sales reps to read industry-focused resources and watch videos to become well versed. To help this journey along, deploy real-world scenarios sooner rather than later. Sales reps learn best by doing something and then practicing it. Reading and watching are never enough. Conduct practice discussions with real customers and invite their honest feedback. It accelerates learning and makes verticalization a more natural sales motion.

Horizontal Use Cases

It can be daunting to think about enabling end-to-end verticalization of an entire sales organization. One way to make it easier is to start by educating sales reps on use cases that act more horizontal in nature. For example, consider how many industries use supply chains or want to develop a customer-360 view. While the specific wording may change, these types of use cases represent an easy place to start because they address more universal challenges. You can enable the entire sales organization because it's the same basic use case across industries, with only some slight differences. This strategy may be less intimidating than diving into industry-specific challenges right off the bat.

Use Your Partners' Industry Experience

Your solution or consulting partners have likely been verticalized for a long time, and they have practices built around vertical go-to-market strategies. They already speak the language of the industry, so it's much more comfortable for them to sell your solution in that language than to learn your horizontal technology language. Verticalization only benefits partner relationships. It's smart to lean on your trusted partners and ask them to help you make sense of where best to target your efforts. They've been in this world longer than you and can provide a gut check on how to handle situations.

Overall, keep two things in mind: Some industries will take significantly longer to penetrate, so you need to be thoughtful about how much energy you're willing to put into a region and the required customer education. Second, some countries and industries might not be the right place to verticalize. Be honest about your chances for success and select accordingly. It's the best way to ensure that verticalization sends your sales . . . well, vertical.

Marketing Hires

A vice president of marketing in EMEA is not the first person you hire. Instead, hire a demand gen/field marketing person. They liaise with similar folks in the United States and get a lot of energy from what's happening at headquarters. They then hire someone else, and so on. So, we had a few people and then a few more people, and at some point, we needed to break that off and make it a separate marketing team for that country. We hired those people first and then hired a vice president. Otherwise, what would a vice president do if they were the first hire?

We grew APJ in the same way. The first person we hired was a demand gen/field marketer who reported to our vice president of demand gen in the United States. The job was essentially a replication of a lot of the things that we had done in the United States. We needed operational support in APJ—that was first and foremost. Over time, and as those organizations grew, we broke Europe off into a separate unit. A year later, APJ broke off, and that became a separate unit with their own marketing vice president. All the while, they're getting the lifeblood of HQ, where we have the knowledge, the proof points and the creative storytelling, which need to be shared with other territories. We created a lot of the templates and campaigns in a box at HQ and exported them to our teams globally. At the same time, there's a lot more localization and local development going on today, versus what we saw just a few years earlier.

17

Alignment for the Ages

"Innovation at full speed. Operating at hyperspeed."
—Chris Degnan

FRANK SLOOTMAN SPENT nearly five years as Snowflake's CEO. He led Snowflake brilliantly through tough and triumphant times and left a mark on the company that will never fade. He announced his departure from the top job the day Snowflake reported nearly $2.8 billion in revenue for its fiscal year ending on January 31, 2024. His successor, Sridhar Ramaswamy, arrived at Snowflake the previous year as cofounder of Neeva, which Snowflake had acquired. Sridhar obtained his undergraduate degree in computer science from the Indian Institute of Technology Madras and his PhD in computer science from Brown University. Prior to Snowflake, he spent 15 years ascending from the role of a software engineer to executive management in the technology industry. Frank spent a great deal of his time focused on sales and marketing. Sridhar is an engineer, a numbers guy, and he wants to boil everything down to a one and a zero. Though he may not know about enterprise sales, he's an amazing operations person and knows how to run efficient organizations such as Snowflake's engineering team. He's all about creating structure and process for scale and is very good at understanding the business, building the right structures and scaling for the future. He was also the obvious choice to lead Snowflake through the generative AI race.

We've always had only one product SKU for Snowflake's AI Data Cloud. It enables a number of core data workloads, such as data warehouses, data engineering, and AI. Just prior to Sridhar's ascendancy, we altered our product marketing strategy in order to highlight key capabilities as featured products of our data platform. A computing platform can mean many things to your target audiences, but you have to expand your message by marketing beyond just the benefits of a platform's architecture. That was Snowflake's original go-to-market strategy and it worked very well in the early days. Then we focused on data workloads. From there, we expanded our focus to include tackling not just technology problems but business problems. We serve a number of vertical industries and their business leaders with solutions and content as to how our platform can solve problems and create opportunities. We also focus on solving the problems of horizontal business functions seen in nearly every company, such as finance, IT, marketing, and cybersecurity. They are similar to the gears of an engine—different shapes and sizes, all finely tuned, perfectly interlocked with each other, and the ability for drivers (customers) to choose the gear they desire based on their needs and the conditions. As with any tech company, for the time being, we continue to add gears (latest capabilities) such as the ability to build generative AI applications that use fully managed large language models (LLMs). In essence, we now have multiple products within our single platform and we're aligned to market and sell those products as such.

To reach $3 billion, $5 billion, or even $10 billion in revenue, your former startup/now public company must continue to innovate and deliver new technologies and features that solve problems and create new business opportunities that customers have yet to encounter or ponder. All the while, you have to stay ahead of your competition. Snowflake's platform had a number of disruptive capabilities baked into it when the product became generally available in 2015. But we could not rest, not for a minute. Bob Muglia said confidently: "The competition will catch up to where we are now in a few years." It also means your sales and marketing organizations must remain as aligned as they were when both teams could still squeeze into one conference room.

Absolute Customer-Centric Alignment

Companies that reach and exceed a billion dollars in annual revenue also reach an inflection point. Executives know they have to continue growing the business but doing so in unison and coordination. Your marketing team will consist of hundreds of employees and sales will have thousands. Both organizations know they have to be innovative but remain aligned in order to deliver a customer-centric go-to-market strategy. But the sheer size of your company requires sales and marketing to remain aligned, while aligning with additional teams such as product and finance to deliver for your customers and your business.

Consider the race every tech company wants to win or least remain in: AI. At Snowflake, there's five or so product technologies we really focus on and AI is one of them. The key to this alignment is product, sales, and marketing agreeing on what matters. On the buy side, who are we marketing to at the decision-making level? It's not the CDO. They don't own the budget for AI. It's line-of-business leaders who want to use AI to do better customer service. Or, it's IT.

You have to realize the buyer is different, so there's a leap you have to make in terms of the people who are your customers. It's who actually uses the features. A data analyst and a data scientist use different tools and different programming languages. In terms of marketing, we have to speak to them in different ways. With AI, everyone is trying so hard to win this air war. Whereas, data warehouses and competitive migrations are more traditional opportunities. We're seeing customers use certain features of our product at a much higher rate than we've anticipated. There's an external motivation to compete on this. We don't need the same message focused on product architecture differentiators that we relied on 10 years ago. We've done that very successfully. So the marketing mix is different. Also, we're entering this new phase of multi-product adoption. Innovation is at full speed. That's the difference now. We have more products to sell. That's also a new challenge for sales and marketing's go-to-market motion. How do you handle new products that your sales and marketing people are not really trained on yet?

On the sales side, reps need to speak in a slightly different language that will resonate with the AI personas and have a different level of technical expertise. With AI in particular, customer personas go really deep, really quickly. So, we need to have sellers who are trained to meet them in those conversations. For Snowflake, it's different skills that you need to train for. On the product and engineering side, an AI engineer building products for Snowflake is going to be different from your classic database engineer.

Executing on Alignment

What does alignment look like on a day-to-day basis, and what does it mean to have marketing, sales, and product wholly dedicated to that alignment at any level of growth or size of your business? How do each of those organizations mirror each other so that they're stronger? In marketing, we still have our original GTM groups that include a person from demand generation, product marketing, content marketing, ABM, and PR. The product marketer remains the conduit between product management and the cross-functional marketing teams.

Now, across Snowflake there is a working group for each of our new product areas. For example, we have an AI group that has a product manager, sales leader, and a product marketer. We have additional folks who join these teams as needed—partner marketers to plug in our partner ecosystem; someone from finance to help forecast, report, and track revenue; and someone from sales strategy for enablement, compensation plans, and other functions from sales operations. Those are the company-level product working groups for each product area. The product marketing manager is the person in those meetings who is also a member of the cross-functional marketing team. Once again, they are the conduit. For example, the product marketer who helps develop our AI strategy within that company-level working group turns to the marketing, cross-functional group and directs that AI execution strategy. It's a powerful and never-ending feedback loop between product strategy teams and their corresponding cross-functional marketing teams. The goal is to avoid the traditional relationship where a marketer just hears things in one-on-one meetings with a product manager or a salesperson. It's a corporate-wide working group with each of the core functions in charge of the go-to-market strategy and reports to our executive leadership team. They are sending a note on a regular cadence to say: "Hey, here's how our business is growing. Here are the concerns. Here's what we need help on. Here's our focus areas for the next six months." And then the product marketer in the room is able to direct and orchestrate across the marketing organization's working group in the same fashion to develop a go-to-market strategy.

On the sales side, the same motion is happening. The sales leaders, who are members of each company-level product working group, transfer the knowledge from these strategy teams back to the sales organization. The sales leader is also the leader of each cross-functional group. That's very intentional, ensuring we're aligned to what will make sales successful and focus on what customers want. That's a shift from a very product-run business. Product builds it, marketing launches it, sales is selling it, and then there's a feedback loop. Sales is either coming back to marketing to say, "Hey, these sales enablement materials from marketing are not working," or they say to the product team, "Hey, the product is not working." It creates more accountability and it's all customer-centric.

What are the deliverables for each team? Ultimately, that product group of three are responsible for revenue of their area. There are leading indicators and KPIs they should be measuring. For example, how many new opportunities are being opened? They're looking at what is the sales pipeline for their area. And they're responsible for specialists to sell it and bring in new business. For the marketers, in relation to AI for example, it's about creating awareness. Revenue is important but making sure we are part of every AI conversation is just as important. So, the marketing outputs are about how we can build campaigns that are going to shift that perception in the market. The role of the marketing organization is still the same—to make sales successful by driving pipeline. The difference is that there's no air between sales and product and marketing as far as the strategy behind that. The marketers are working on what their campaigns will be for the first six months of the year. Product is that constant feedback loop: How can we improve the product and how can we launch these products more effectively into the market? Sales takes everything from product and marketing to build its strategy of selling to new and existing customer opportunities.

Looking Back to Launch Forward

The two of us worked together, day after day, for more than nine years. Individually, we remained focused on our customer-centric vision, while always asking, "What's next?" We have hired the best people we could find and put them in the right jobs at the right time. As we've said, we often choose aptitude over experience. When either one of us made a hiring mistake, those people moved on when it was their time. Almost always they made that decision. Along the way, we helped our employees grow in their careers and advance within our teams. As leaders, we've never stopped learning from those who walked our journey before us. As leaders, we've built, assessed and restructured our organizations to reveal what's new and possible with our technology, and to best serve existing customers and engage new audiences and their companies. We rolled up our sleeves when needed and expected from others what we ourselves continued to deliver to our company. We remained vigilant as the world hoped and waited for the pandemic to pass. We mustered our teams virtually so business could continue as usual. We recognized what worked but spent much more time scrutinizing what didn't. We remained humble in an industry, time, and place where big egos are often encouraged.

As a duo, we respect each other, knowing we could come to the other with any issue. We talked most days. Our pursuit of alignment between both of our organizations never ended. No amount of success impeded that goal. We always looked for new ways to align within and between our organizations, and with other Snowflake teams to serve our customers and our business. If any connection was out of alignment, we found it and fixed it. When something went wrong, we owned it as individuals or together as a team. We didn't stand for finger-pointing, gossip, or blame games. We went direct and required that everyone in each of our organizations did too. We praised success but spent much more time revealing and remedying what was broken. If we had an issue with someone in the other person's team, we told each other. If we thought it was time they exit Snowflake, we told each other that too. We floored the accelerator more often than we pumped the brakes. We each knew our place at Snowflake and that of our teams: marketing serves sales so sales can serve our customers. We focused on our strengths when our CEO had the same or different strengths. We found the value in their leadership and management styles, but we may have also scrutinized based on evidence. We knew why they were in the top job when they were in the top job. We were each on a rolling, three-month work contract, in our own minds. We were always interviewing for the job we already had, and we were good with that.

We always had brilliant executive leadership and ingenious engineering, product and finance teams. Snowflake's success rests on everyone in the company. Over the years, the two of us have been asked consistently, "How do you do it?" How does Snowflake sales and marketing continue to attract customers and drive revenue in ways that many other companies can't? "Absolute alignment," is often our answer. It's not just something we wrote on a wall, thinking that will affect change. We commit to it, strategize for it, and then deliver on it.

We hope you gained incredible value from this book. We crafted it so others could learn how Snowflake's sales and marketing teams helped vault the company from a ground-zero startup to a multi-billion dollar tech powerhouse in less than 10 years. It always has been and always will be about alignment and every success that comes from that.

Acknowledgments

So many individuals have taught, inspired, and entrusted us before and during our careers. We are grateful to those who gave us the insights and support we needed so dearly as young professionals. Working hard and staying hungry without the advice from those who journeyed before you remain moot endeavors. We're also grateful for those who taught us to be humble, and remain humble. It's a rare leadership quality. Without it, we would not have developed our constant hunger for knowledge. They are the heads and tails of a coin, the front and back of a hand. Hunger and humility: one can't exist without the other.

We also want to thank everyone who took a chance on us to help lead Snowflake. We had success at our prior companies, but that doesn't diminish the risk involved when hiring anyone to help lead a startup. When each of us arrived, and thereafter, we had the support of Snowflake's founders and board members, its three successive CEOs, and all of those who have worked for us and brought their best game to Snowflake, day in and day out. We are also grateful to Snowflake's customers. Being constantly in their service is what drives us to do what we do. Snowflake's business partners are also worthy of praise. They have been an inspiration to, and extension of, our sales and marketing strategy and execution since day one.

This book could not have been possible without everyone who helped bring it to life. Thank you to our founding investor, Mike Speiser, for inviting us to help his vision become reality. Thanks to all past and present employees who took time out to provide input on what became our final draft. We are also grateful to our publisher, Wiley & Sons. They guided us through the entire editorial process and provided resources and support when and where we needed them. We also want to thank editor and writer Roger Scholl, for jump-starting the editorial process with early interviews and chapter drafts. This book also wouldn't be possible without the writing, editing, and interviewing efforts of Vince Morello, who worked for Snowflake for most of the years that this book covers. He jump-started Snowflake's content marketing and thought leadership efforts, and later became Snowflake's chief storyteller.

Lastly, we want to recognize our families. Silicon Valley startups are huge career risks that garner less salary compared to what's available when working for global, veteran software companies. Then there's the crazy schedules, buoyed by intense competition and the constant need to keep delivering and staying relevant. Our families have always been there, and doing even more to support us during uncertain times. When the success did come, they kept it real by reminding us who we were, and still are, before Snowflake took off like a rocket. For that, we will remain eternally grateful. Lastly, we want to thank each other. Our working relationship has defied the industry standard. That's only possible through focus, respect, and a shared vision of developing and maintaining absolute alignment between our sales and marketing organizations.

NOW IT'S TIME TO GO-TO-MARKET.

Visit MakeItSnow.com

Align your marketing and sales teams with:
- Media
- Resources
- Case Studies
- and more support

Learn, build, and connect with us.

MakeItSnowBook.com

Index

80-20 curse, 65

A
Account-based marketing (ABM),
    86–88, 130–131, 189
  outbound ABM programs, 156
  SDR alignment, 86, 168–169
  strategy, usage, 88
  tiers, 86–87
Account executives (AEs),
    experience (value), 163
Account propensity score (APS),
    building, 115
Adversaries, selection/business
    win, 45–47
AI Data Cloud, 168, 208
Alignment, 207
  cascading, 123–124
  cross-functional alignment,
    mastery, 141
  establishment, 122–123
  execution, 125, 210–211
  importance, 105, 212–213
  problems, 132
Alliances, jumpstarting, 53–54
Amazon Web Services (AWS)
  cloud computing dominance, 42
  data storage, commission
    charge, 56
  partnership, 57
  re:Invent conference, Redshift
    announcement, 56
Amp It Up (Slootman), 160
Annual customer engagement
    survey, initiation, 95
Annual recurring revenue (ARR),
    booking, 107
Application programming interfaces
    (APIs), customer usage, 55
Application sprawl, 97
Aptitude, hiring choice, 142
Artificial intelligence (AI)
  nonusage, 97–98
  products, 182

Artificial intelligence (*continued*)
   pursuit, 16
   usage, 114, 209–210
Asia Pacific and Japan (APJ), 192–201
Automation
   barriers, removal, 174
   resources, need, 121
   software, usage, 97
   strategic initiative, 121

B

Baseless claims, avoidance, 64
Beliefs (support), evidence (need), 32
BigQuery (Google), competition, 55
Bilateral communication, 199
Billboard space, search/advertisement, 99–101
Board of directors, depth, 8–10
Boldness
   delivery, 104–105
   importance, 98–101
Bottom-up sales, 163
Brand
   development, 186
   experience, positioning (link), 98
   marketing, 185–186
   success, 92–95
Brand awareness
   challenge, 98
   customer advocacy, impact, 83
Budgetary alignment, 105
"Build for a billion" (Muglia), 149
Burnout, 65
Business automation, 158
Business ecosystems
   partners, importance, 145
   scale, origin, 53

Business intelligence (BI)
   partnerships, 54–56
   solution providers, relationships (cementing), 86
   tools, 36, 49
Business problems, 208
Business-to-business (B2B) data provider, data delivery, 115
Business-to-business (B2B) software, impact, 165

C

Campaigns, activation, 129
Candidates, selection, 30
Championing, 38
Chestnut, Ken, 56, 59
Chief Executive Officers (CEOs)
   perspectives, 159
   product pivot, 157–158
   sales duties, 153–154
   visionary, requirement, 158
Chief Marketing Officer (CMO)
   characteristics, 74–75
   sales leads, generation, 77–78
   types, 122
Chief Revenue Officer (CRO)
   position, 164
   selection, hiring/promotion question, 116–117
Christensen, Lars, 78–80, 97–98
Cloud-built data platform, capabilities, 182
Cloud computing, resources, 42
Cloud data platform messaging, 157
Cloud data warehouse, customer migration, 113
Cloud infrastructure providers, relationships (cementing), 86
Cloud-native customers, focus, 35

Cloud storage, 177
Cloud strategy, development, 49
Commercial sales team, 171
Community marketing, 183–185
Company
  course correction, 109
  culture, jumpstarting, 12–14
  pain points, identification, 38
  values, 62–63, 70, 146
Company-wide editorial process, need, 79
Compensation packages, negotiation, 30
Competition
  identification, 38
  market force, 134
  disruption reaction, 161
  salespeople hiring, 33–34
  targeting, 41
  total addressable market (TAM), competitor share, 46
Conflict, culture, 76
Consistency, importance, 98
Constant learning, motivation, 10
Constructive debate, integrity (existence), 66
Consumption-based pricing, 50–52
Consumption-based product, 63, 112
Content delivery, 184–185
Content marketing, 79–81
  jumpstarting, 80
  leader, partnership, 78
Continuity, importance, 136
Cross-functional alignment, mastery, 141
Cross-functional teams, establishment, 189–190

Cruanes, Thierry, 5, 70
  feedback, 20
  problem solving, 11
  prospect interaction, 23
Culture
  embedding, 3
  establishment, 158
  scaling, 61
Customer 360, 177, 203
Customer-centric alignment, 209–210
Customer-centric marketing, 94–96, 104
Customer relationship management (CRM)
  data, usage, 203
  platform, 96–97
  solution, 170
    data platform, contrast, 115
Customers
  advocacy, impact, 83
  awareness, creation, 120
  cloud-native customers, focus, 35
  decision process, 37
  engagement, 153
  feedback, 179
  focus, 95–96, 112–113
  happiness, impact, 180–181
  influence, persona development, 95
  legacy solution, migration, 53
  live events, impact, 83
  marketing, 82–83
  problems, solving, 24, 35
  references, requests, 98
  regression, sales funnel examination, 84–85
  wins/losses, 48
Customer Success team, establishment, 95–96

D

Dageville, Benoit, 5, 70
  feedback, 20
  problem solving, 11
  prospect interaction, 23
  startup perspective, 42
Data
  collection tools, 170
  encryption, 36
  enrichment, 115
  insights, 113–114
  loads, control, 49
  migration, 46
  pipeline, data engineer control, 20
  platform, building, 133
  sharing, 115, 178
  storage, 110–111
  warehousing, 126
  workloads, handling/focus, 133, 208
Database, optimizing/building, 79
Data-driven marketing organization, scaling, 173
Data-driven plan, usage, 200
Data for Breakfast, usage, 127
Deals, size (increase), 47–50
Decision process, knowledge, 37
Degnan, Chris, 95, 116
Delivery
  commitment, 68
  ensuring, 66–67
Demand generation (demand gen), 22–23, 76, 125–129
  campaigns, content offering, 80–81
  function, 75, 120
  partnering, 185
  process, automation/scaling, 97–98
  requirements, 79
  SDR, relationship, 169–170
Developer marketing, 183–185
Differences, embracing, 68
Direct customer model, 199
Disagreement, integrity (existence), 66
Disillusionment, 38–39
"Drinking your own champagne" metaphor, 179–180
Dunkel, Dick, 36
Dysfunction, creation, 125

E

Economic buyer, identification, 37
Ecosystem, importance, 59
Email templates, usage, 170–171
EMEA, 192–201
Employee
  commitment, delivery, 67–68
  departure, 147
  morale, increase, 99
  retention, strengths (capitalization), 144–145
Engineering, sales (alignment), 11–12
Engineers, feedback (usage), 23
Enterprise sales team, 151, 171
Enterprise solution, offering, 119–120
Evaluation agreements, sale, 29
Events, community attraction, 185
Evidence-based questions, value (conveyance), 64
Executive communications, impact, 187–189
Executive referrals, 143–144
Executives, selection, 10–11

F

Feedback, 6–7, 95
  receiving, 10–11, 167, 179
  usage, 23
Field marketing, 83–85
Field sales infrastructure, placement, 130
Financial metrics, driving, 104
First hires, 76–77
Forecasts, sales/marketing team discussion, 131–132
Founders, core expertise focus, 11
Franchises, 127–129
Functionality, incorporation, 35

G

General availability (GA), 6, 22–23, 45–46
  alliances, jumpstarting, 53–54
  approach, 61–62, 89, 191
  sales motions, 47–48
Generative AI, pursuit, 16, 207
Global expansion, steps, 191–196
Google Cloud Platform, 57, 59, 111
Go-to-market (GTM)
  groups, presence, 210
  practices, 174
  strategy/approach, 54–56, 152, 187, 198–199, 211
  teams, program/campaign planning, 189–190
Griffith DeMartini, Caitlin 84
Growth, sales team (restructuring), 150–151

H

Head of sales, hiring, 6
Health Insurance Portability and Accountability Act (HIPAA) customer compliance, support, 110
  requirements, enterprise compliance, 36
"Healthy tension," impact, 102
High-level candidate, rejection, 143–144
Hiring, 139
  expert, hiring, 29–30
  first hires, 76–77
  local hiring, 198
  process, importance, 27–29
Horizontal use cases, impact, 203–204
Human resources (HR), demand gen usage, 126–127

I

Ideal customer profile (ICP), creation/development, 9, 19–20
Identification (company pain points), 38
Inbound demand, response, 163–164
Inbound requests, tracking, 174
Incoming demand, handling, 103
Initial public offering (IPO), 83
Innate attributes, importance, 144
Inside sales team, 151
Integrity
  importance, 64
  presence, 142
  value, 66
Integrity-infused workplace, meaning, 64
Intelligence/humility, combination (importance), 142
Interviews, 82–83

J

Jassy, Andy, 56
Joint marketing programs, message, 85–86

K

Key performance indicators (KPIs), usage, 211

L

Large language model (LLM), 167, 208
Leaders, Snowflake hiring, 143
Leading indicators, measurement, 211
Leads, 169
　flow, increase, 78
　generation, 124
　quality/quantity, 102
Legacy
　migration, value, 50
　systems, construction, 23
　vendors, competition (absence), 152
Legacy products
　data migration, 46
　flattening, 28–29
Live events, impact, 83
Local workshops, online transfer, 98

M

Machine learning (ML)
　pursuit, 16
　usage, 114
Majors sales team, 151, 171
　vertical sales element, addition, 152
"Manage down, not up" (Slootman), 160
Management layers, evolution, 30

Market
　category, defining, 93
　forces, impact, 133–134
　maturity, 201
　opportunity, 94
　position, 91–94
　target market, identification, 103–104
Marketing, 73
　absence, 82
　analytics, usage, 97
　automation, types (identification), 96–97
　campaigns, evaluation, 145
　channels, messages, 95
　CMO approach, 75
　customer-centric marketing team, achievement, 94–96
　data stack, 176
　efficiency, 101–102
　events, delivery, 85
　functions, 75, 78
　hires, global usage, 204–205
　impact, 124–125
　joint marketing programs, message, 85–86
　operations
　　deployment, 78
　　establishment, 175
　organization, 189
　partner marketing, 85–86, 129–130
　product management, alignment, 102
　purpose, 81
　relationship, 130
　sales
　　alignment, 119
　　development, transfer, 155–156

scoring model, 131–132
tools, 156
Marketing automation platform (MAP), 96–97
Marketing pillars, 91
  creation, 92
  establishment, 103–105
  types, 92–103
Marketing teams
  creation/scaling, 181–189
  edge, requirement, 81
  evolution, 183
  growth/delivery, 173–174
Mass-marketing channels, usage, 126
McMahon, John, 8–9
  CRO perspective, 44
  customer purchase advice, 22
  global expansion, control, 192
  hiring advice, 116
  meetings, regularity, 25
  Snowflake opportunities, discussion, 35–36
MEDDPICC sales qualification, 36–38, 108
Messaging, concentration, 130–131
Metrics, usage/clarity, 37
Microsoft Azure, 57–59, 111
Microsoft Partner Network, 59
Migration
  guides, development, 34
  time consumption, 46
Mindshare, building, 91
Misalignment, presence, 124, 125
Modern Marketing Data Stack report, 176
Morello, Vince, 80–81
Muglia, Bob, 8, 9, 116, 181
  "build for a billion," 149
  impact, 43–44, 61, 187
  value, 152

Multi-clustered shared data architecture, term (coining), 21
Munir, Abdul, 12
Mustafa, Saqib, 85

N

Nadell, Satya, 59
Napoli, Jack, 36
Net promoter score (NPS), obtaining/usage, 95
Networking, 140

O

Objectives and Key Results (OKRs), sharing, 123
Onboarding, 156
One-to-few strategy, 131
One-to-many approach, 87
One-to-one ABM experience, delivery, 87
On-premises computing, shift, 35
Outbound campaigns, usage, 126
Outbound cold calling, 156
Outside-in approach, 104

P

Paper process, awareness, 37
Partner-led markets, 202
Partner marketing, 85–86, 129–130
Partners
  global considerations, 199
  industry experience, usage, 204
  marketing relationship, 130
  scaling, 53
  serving, 105
  training, 113
Peets, Chad, 4, 29–30, 155
People/values, alignment (absence), 69–70

Performance (company characteristic), 94
Persson, Denise (Snowflake employment/hiring), 9–10, 19, 78
Pilot programs, usage, 202
Pipelines
   building, 155–156
   management, 180
   sales/marketing team discussion, 131–132
Platform, examination, 158–159
Positioning
   brand experience, link, 98
   exercise, 134
   question, 103–104
Positioning (Ries), 92
Post-GA product, features (absence), 24
Pre-GA product, features (absence), 24
Pre-IPO stock options, equity form, 64
Press releases, development, 80
Product
   advancement, 200
   development, progression, 18
   differentiation, determination, 16–18, 92–93
   experience, 121
   features/functionality, delivery, 63
   management, marketing (alignment), 102
   marketers, impact, 6–7
   offering, expansion, 168
   positioning, 133–134
   presentation, delivery, 7–8
Productivity model, 108–109
Product manager
   impact, 6–7
   job, 22–24
   success, importance, 28
Product marketing, 181–183
   background, importance, 122
   strategy, alteration, 208
   success, 135–136
   team, vertical/industry marketing (inclusion), 182
Professional services organization, establishment, 112–114
Profitability, success output, 104
Proof of concept (POC), conducting, 57–58
Prospects
   data/insights, requirement, 92
   identification, 126
   intent, basis, 167–168
Public relations (PR), 88–89, 188
Pull effect, 192–193

Q

Qualified Sales Leader, The (McMahon), 8–9
Quarterly results system ("What Matters"), deployment, 89, 123

R

Ramaswamy, Sridhar, 207
Reach (partner marketing reason), 129
Recruitment, snowboards (usage), 99
Retention, 139
Revenue growth, 101–102, 104
Ries, Al, 92
Rouke, Kyle, 27–29

S

SaaS products
  leverage, 87
  subscription, 97
Sales
  alignment, 101–103
  annual quotas, success, 155
  deals, complexity (increase), 114
  development, transfer, 155–156
  efficiency, marketing (impact), 124–125
  embedding, 3
  enablement, 108, 135–136, 203
  engineering, alignment, 11–12
  engineer scaling, 110–111
  engineers, importance, 34
  experience, acquisition, 19
  focus, 29
  funnel, 84–85, 120
  head of sales, hiring, 6
  leaders, CMO generation, 77–78
  marketing, alignment, 119
  operations, delay (mistake), 114–115
  opportunities, generation, 86–87
  organization, tiers, 171
  patience/focus/humility, 24–26
  pipeline, building, 155–156
  pitch, development, 20–22
  strategy, development, 15
  stress, 33
Sales development representatives (SDRs), 103
  ABM, alignment, 86, 168–169
  account executive, relationship, 167
  demand generation, relationship, 169–170
  deployment, 171
  follow-ups, 132
  function, 84, 192
  importance, 164–165
  lead generation, 124
  lead measurement, 155–156
  mission, 163
  onboarding, 167
  prospecting activity, 156
  selection/development, 165–167
  skills, building, 166
  success, metrics, 172
  support ratio, creation, 109
  tech stack reliance, 170–171
  work plan, 164–165
Sales representatives
  culture/company values, 70
  hiring, 33–34
  deployment, 27, 201
  leading by example, 34
  leading, learning, 111–112
  need, understanding, 84
  profiles, 31–33
  accountability, 34
  advancement, 107
  demand generation function, running, 120
  friction, 114
  near-zero attrition, 107
  restructuring, 150–151
  SDR support, 171
  structure, reorganization, 151
Scaling
  importance, 174
  initiation, 96–98
  partner marketing reason, 129
  self-scaling, 140–141
Scarpelli, Mike, 155
Simplicity (company characteristic), 94

Slootman, Frank, 149–151, 187
   all-hands meeting, 65
   business value, 152
   strategy, execution
     (relationship), 77
   value, 150–155, 160, 207
Snowboards, impact, 99
Snowflake
   architecture, uniqueness, 43
   AWS infrastructure, usage, 57
   blog strategy, 188
   Build conference, 128
   business benefits, customer
     discussion, 82
   community, size, 184
   customer-led company, 123
   customer selection, meaning, 58
   deals, size (increase), 47–50
   engineers, impact (McMahon
     perspective), 50
   global expansion, 191
   initiatives, 78
   internal promotions, 111–112
   launch, 58–59, 212–213
   leadership team, input, 93
   market awareness, 180–181
   marketing team
     functions, 122
   program development, 47
   partner program, management, 65
   platform, positioning, 19
   positioning, reciprocation, 134
   product development, progression, 18–19
   rebranding, 133–134
   repositioning, 181–182
   sales
     considerations, 134–135
     kickoff event, 45
     skills/experiences,
       requirements, 150
   Summit (conference), 127–129
   usage, ease/power, 17–18
   values, 63–68
     accountability, 68–69
   workloads, addition, 135
Snowflake Sales Development
   Academy (microsite),
   166–167
Snowflake World Tour, initiation, 128
Social media, usage, 126
Software engineers, focus, 12
Software technology, intelligence
   requirement, 142–143
Sonic booms, 127–129,
   189–190
Speiser, Mike, 5–6, 28, 116
   engineering teams, assembling, 70
   triple, triple, triple, double,
     double strategy, 65
Startups
   challenges, 88
   customer, connection advice, 35
   growth
     deceleration, 174
     sales professionals,
       involvement, 33
   marketing, customer
     importance, 96
   sales/culture, embedding, 3
   stealth mode, 28
   work ethic, 159
Strategy
   defining, data (usage), 203
   development/execution,
     importance, 66–67
   execution, relationship, 77
Strengths, capitalization/
   leveraging, 144–145
Summit (Snowflake user
   conference),
   127–128

T

Tableau, partnership, 55–56
Targeted ads, launch, 87
Target market, identification, 103–104
Team, building, 75–76
Technical decision-makers, impact, 12
Technology
    companies, relationships (cementing), 86
    disruptive approach, value, 11
    problems, 208
    sales ability, 32–33
Teradata, 46, 47, 113
    cloud offering, 85
    targeting, 47, 101
Thought leadership marketing, 80–81
Total addressable market (TAM), 46, 202
Touchpoints, story (consistency), 93
Training, 156
    MEDDPICC sales qualification process, usage, 36–38
Triple, triple, triple, double, double strategy, 65
    completion, 107
Trotta, Vince, 27–29
    Reshift account perspective, 44–45
Trust
    building
        consistency, impact, 92–93
        initiation, 120–122
    leader/management trust, 119–120

V

Value-based information/insights, providing, 126
Values
    alignment, absence, 69–70, 76
    creation, 62–63
    importance, 139
    review, frequency, 69
Vendor, accountability problems, 52
Venezia, Nancy, 13
Venture capital investor, sharing, 54
Vertica, 46, 50
Verticalization, 200–202
Vertical marketing strategy, absence, 83
Virgin America, airline industry disruption, 98
Virtual cockpit, usage, 166
Virtual salesforce (creation), partnerships (impact), 54–56

W

Website
    stress testing, 126
    traffic (increase), marketing (responsibility), 122
Whale hunters (enterprise sales reps), recruitment (avoidance), 35
"What Matters" (quarterly results system), deployment, 89, 123
Work ethic, 140, 145–146, 159
"Working at speed," 145–146

Z

Zero-management pitch, 21
Zukowski, Marcin, 5